954
783   9841
P9-DOG-561

FAVORITE BIRDS OF FLORIDA

WRITTEN BY
DICK SCHINKEL

ILLUSTRATED BY
DAVID MOHRHARDT

With 125 full-color illustrations

Holt, Michigan

Copyright © 1995 by Thunder Bay Press

All rights reserved. No part of this book may be used or reproduced in any
manner without prior written permission of the publisher, except in the case of
brief quotations emboded in ciritcal reviews and articles.

95 96 97 98 99   1 2 3 4 5 6 7 8

Illustrations by David Mohrhardt
Edited by Maureen MacLaughlin-Morris
Prepress by Advanced Imaging
Printed in Hong Kong by Everbest for
Four Colour Imports, Ltd.
Logo design by Lynda A. Bass

ISBN: 1-882376-22-6

Holt, Michigan

To Larry West, nature photographer nonpareil,
and to Al and Rory Curtenius. Their generosity
helped make the artwork for this book possible.

INTRODUCTION

Florida is an extremely popular state for vacations with its great amount of shoreline and wetlands. This coupled with the fact that the peninsula is the closest thing the United States has to a tropical climate means that Florida offers a dramatic variety of habitat diversity. There are forests, brush and scrub lands, swamps, marshes, fallow fields, prairies, agricultural lands, shorelines, pelagic areas and a variety of habitats inbetween.

During the winter the human population of Florida is greatly increased by "Snowbirds," northern residents leaving the bitter weather for a warm and balmy climate. Most visits to Florida will be during the cooler periods of fall, winter and early spring which is a good time to see birds that are winter residents and permanent residents, many of which are found nowhere else in the United States. Florida is rich with natural areas, state parks and national recreational areas. Many Florida resorts, motels and charters are catering to the natural history and birding public. Whereas in the past birdwatching was looked upon as sort of an oddity, today all natural areas, parks and reserves welcome birders.

Being a very long state, bird populations and diversity can be very different from the north to the south and from habitat to habitat. The north and panhandle of Florida are very similar to the states that surround it but as you go further south into the subtropical areas of south Florida, the populations change as well as vegetation. In the Keys or the Dry Tortugas, you can expect birds of a very tropical nature. During the summer breeding season, the Keys and south Florida are host to a variety of tropical species and unless you travel to Mexico or Central America you will not see them at all. Migration times are also an opportunity to see a variety of birds, especially during the spring when many birds will be going into their breeding plumage.

The intent of this book is to provide a reference for those birds encountered in Florida as well as those a beginning birder may seek out because of the uniqueness of the state. This book will not attempt to cover all three hundred plus species of birds that may be found in Florida, but it will cover those that attract the attention of the beginning birder and that can be found in the most-visited places in the state. In many cases, plumages of different seasons are given because these can, and usually will, be represented at one time of the year or another. The topography of a bird is given to help in identifications.

The birds discussed this text are fairly easily found in the correct habitat at the proper time of the year. It is recommended that a diary to kept in this book by writing where and when you first sight a bird on the page that the bird is listed. This will come in handy in years to come in remembering places and events. This practice is very rewarding and is similar to keeping a family album. Indeed, these birds will become part of your family.

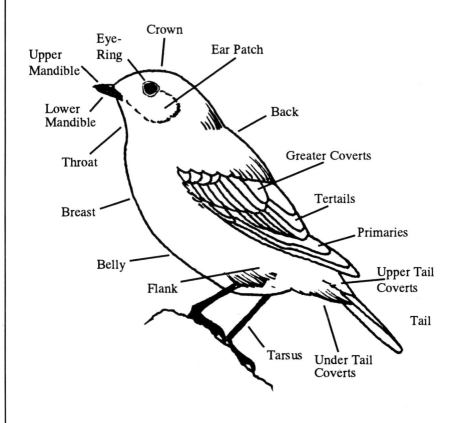

Upper Mandible

Eye-Ring

Crown

Ear Patch

Lower Mandible

Throat

Back

Breast

Greater Coverts

Tertails

Primaries

Belly

Flank

Upper Tail Coverts

Tail

Tarsus

Under Tail Coverts

TOPOGRAPHY OF A BIRD

Pied-billed Grebe   *Podilymbus podiceps*

Although the Pied-billed Grebe breeds in the state of Florida it is most common during the winter when the state is inundated with migrants. During the winter it is brown overall with a yellow bill, yellow eye-ring and whitish chin and throat. This bird can be seen in almost any body of water whether it be fresh, salt or brackish. It will float along and dive for fish and small crustaceans or may just submerge itself from a full floating position or to any stage of submerged body.

During the breeding season the bill will be white with a black band around it and a black chin and the throat will be evident. The eye-ring will be white and the light-brown body will be a darker brown. A shallow, floating platform of vegetation is used as a nest. It is anchored among rushes or reeds in open water for protection. The outer part of the nest may contain a ring of green duckweed, algae or pond weeds that the bird may reach while incubating the eggs.

The four or five eggs will hatch in a little over three weeks. The chicks are quite striking, with pronounced streaking appearing almost zebra-like with black-and-white stripes. After a short time (usually a day) the chicks are able to follow the parents and will ride upon the parent's backs. After a month or so the chicks will go through rapid growth and change and soon will be able to leave the parents, although they will remain together as a family group for a while longer. Nesting can occur from early March through late fall, although most nesting is usually complete by September.

During the non-breeding season the Pied-billed Grebe will be mostly solitary or in small loose groups, feeding in open water. A very poor flier, the Grebe will dive to hide itself and appear with only its head above water to assess the situation. It can swim a great distance under water to escape predation. If you are near the Pied-billed Grebe in the water it will not appear overly concerned but each time it dives it will appear just a little further away from you than when it submerged.

The calls of this small bird are not characteristic of its size but more characteristic of marsh birds who must be loud to be heard. The call is similar to that of the Cuckoos. The call starts rather fast and slows down as it finishes its song. The call starts with the *coo coo coo* and then goes into a *cow cow cow* finishing to a slower paced *kup kup kup kup*. This call can be heard in breeding season at any time of day or night.

Pied-billed Grebe

Brown and American White Pelican

Pelecanus occidentalis and Pelecanus erythrorhynchos

Every school child knows the large bird with the pouch, the Pelican. In Florida two species of Pelican are present, the American White Pelican and the Brown Pelican. With a wingspan reaching nearly ten feet the Pelican is quite an impressive bird, and is common on the coasts and waterways of Florida. The White Pelican is quite abundant during the winter months as a winter resident while the Brown Pelican breeds in Florida. The Brown Pelican is more common along the coastline but occasionally can be found on inland lakes and waterways.

The American White Pelican breeds in the middle of the North American continent into the prairies of Canada and winters on the coasts of Florida. Unlike egrets, these large, white birds have black wingtips when flying. When feeding the White Pelicans swim along, usually in groups, thrusting their heads simultaneously into colonies of small fish filling their pouch with water and fish. After pulling their heads above water, the water escapes from the pouch through a narrow slit between the two bills trapping the fish inside. The bill is then tilted upward and the fish swallowed.

The Brown Pelican feeds entirely differently. It dives into the water from the air engulfing fish with its large bill and pouch. It then bobs to the surface and allows the water to drain from its down-turned bill until it can raise its head and swallow the captive fish. The Brown Pelican feeds solitarily or in small, loose groups. The Brown Pelican is not particularly afraid of man so it is found feeding from docks and piers along many waterways, especially where fishermen discard fish entrails. If you happen to find an area where the pelican is diving and you can snorkel it is quite a sight to see them plunge into the water just ahead of you. Snorkelers may actually encourage the pelicans by disturbing schools of fish for them to feed upon.

Brown Pelicans usually lay two to three white eggs. They build a nest in trees or mangroves but may nest on the ground as the American White Pelican does. The eggs will hatch in four to five weeks, with the White Pelican taking longer. The time from hatching to leaving the nest varies on the food supply but usually it is several months.

During the time that DDT was in use the Brown Pelican was in extreme danger of extinction. The DDT caused the eggshells to become soft and break in the nest before hatching. At the time DDT was declared illegal, Florida held the only hope for the Brown Pelican. The population has come back in grand form, although habitat loss is still a concern.

Brown and American White Pelican

Magnificent Frigatebird *Fregata magnificens*

This large seabird is found mainly along the seacoasts of Florida. Only on rare occasions is it found inland and then usually after major storms. This large seabird has even been blown as far inland as the Great Lakes following hurricanes. A tropical bird, the Magnificent Frigatebird is most abundant on the southern coasts of Florida, becoming less common as you travel up the coasts. The Gulf of Mexico coastline seems to have more of these large birds further north than does the Atlantic coast.

The Frigatebird is black with a seven-foot wingspan, pointed wings and forked, pointed tail. The female has a white chest and breast. The bill is long and hooked. The male has a red, inflatable pouch under the chin which is used to attract females. Rarely does the male fly with the pouch inflated. This seabird flies effortlessly along the coastline feeding upon scraps on the water or taking things from the beach.

The Frigatebird does not land to take food, even over water. It dips down and grabs the food with its hooked bill. It will even take crabs and small turtles on the beach in this manner. The Frigatebird is quite adept at stealing the food from other seabirds, harassing them until they drop the food they are carrying or regurgitate it. Many times you will see this beautiful bird riding the offshore wind seemingly almost motionless, hovering over potential food sources.

Being a tropical bird it only nests in the extreme southern Keys and Dry Tortugas. The nest is built by the female with material provided by the male from the mangrove plants, low shrubs and trees. The male selects a branch on a mangrove and inflates its bright-red pouch, waving it back and forth to attract a female from the air. Once a female selects a male she will sit beside him and they will take a few days to bond. Often the male will cover the female with his wing during this bonding period.

One white egg is laid on the small, loose nest and takes over seven weeks to hatch. Both parents will take care of the young for the first three months but the female will finish caring for the young sometimes up to six months to a year. The young birds will have a light-colored head instead of the black of the parents. On the nest, which is usually in a colony, the Frigatebird is not especially wary and will allow you to photograph them from a relatively close range. As in all birds on nests, be cautious not to cause any stress or excitement to the parents or young. This excitement can cause serious difficulties for the young, even death.

Magnificent Frigatebird
Male (left)   Female (right)

Double-crested Cormorant *Phalacrocorax auritus*

The Double-crested Cormorant is called this because of the two plumes or crests that arise from the eye-line during the breeding season. Many people who have never had a close look at this bird during the breeding season think that the double crest comes from the flight silhouette the neck gives to the head. It appears that the head has a slight crest coming from the back much like that of a Cardinal.

The Double-crested Cormorant is black all over and stands about three feet tall. Adult birds have orange throat pouches during the entire year. Immature birds have light-colored throats and chests. The bill of the Cormorant is hooked at the end to catch fish. The Cormorant flies with its neck outstretched with a little bend, whereas the Common Loon, which sometimes can be confused with the Cormorant, flies with its head below the body.

The Double-crested Cormorant is common on the coastline where it feeds on fish. It can be found resting on piers, shrubs, rocks and buildings. It can be seen drying its outstretched wings after swimming for fish. This is similar to the Anhinga except the Cormorant is entirely black where the Anhinga has white shoulders. Populations are on the increase in Florida as well as throughout many parts of the United States, especially in the interior. During the winter, the Florida population is increased by the influx of northern migrants. While in migration the Cormorant will fly in a "V" formation much like Canada Geese.

In Florida the nesting of Cormorants occurs mainly in colonies with herons and storks. Their nests are built in trees and mangroves. Three or four bluish-tinted eggs are laid in the nests and are incubated for about four weeks. They take another five to six weeks to fledge. The young need brooding for about two weeks before being left alone while the parents feed. The young are fed regurgitated fish: first nearly digested liquid, later fish pieces, and finally whole small fish.

The Double-crested Cormorant is quite successful at diving to catch fish. You may see them swimming along with just their head above water slowly sinking from sight. In some areas the increase of Cormorants has caused concern over the decrease in fish populations. This occurs mainly in freshwater areas.

As in many of the birds that are dependant on fish for a living, the Cormorant populations were hurt dramatically when DDT was in unsupervised use. With the ban on DDT, hard pesticides and unnatural chemicals the waters of the lakes and oceans have seen a remarkable population comeback occur especially in the interior of the United States.

Double-crested Cormorant

Anhinga   *Anhinga anhinga*

The Anhinga, or Water Turkey as it is sometimes called, can be found throughout Florida, especially inland on fresh and brackish waters. Less commonly it is found along the coast and panhandle of Florida. Except during the winter when migrants appear, the Keys are fairly devoid of the Anhinga.

The male is black all over except for the white shoulders and upper wings. The female has a buff-brown neck instead of black. The Anhinga is similar to the Cormorant in shape and size. Major differences are in the sharp-pointed bill of the Anhinga as opposed to the hooked bill of the Cormorant. The Anhinga has a longer and much slimmer neck than the Cormorant and its tail is much longer. The feathers of the Anhinga are not as waterproof which allows it to be able to dive and swim after fish with relative ease. Because the feathers get quite wet, the most common pose you will see is the Anhinga with its wings spread and drying.

The Anhinga feeds upon aquatic animals, impaling them with their sharp bill, bringing them to the surface, flipping the prey into the air and swallowing it. Fish and larger prey are usually swallowed head first. The Anhinga, like the Loon and the Cormorant, can submerge itself and swim around with only head and neck above water. This allows the Anhinga to capture fish and invertebrates. This habit of swimming around with only its neck out of the water has given it the name of "Snake Bird."

A nest of loose sticks is built by both sexes, usually in low shrubs or trees such as mangrove and willows, although they can be built in taller trees. Many times the colonial nests are built together with herons, ibis and egrets. Three to six bluish-white eggs are laid in the nest and tended by both sexes. Four weeks of incubation is required to hatch the eggs. The time of fledging is quite variable, dependent upon the food supply and number of chicks in the nest, but can last for four to six weeks. As the young near fledging they will begin to move around with the aid of their feet, wings and bill. Nesting usually begins during March and will continue through June.

The Anhinga is the perfect symbol of Florida's freshwater areas. Any sunny day you will be able to see the Anhinga sitting in the sun drying itself or perhaps see the snake-like head and bill pushing itself through the water before it disappears out of sight in search of prey.

The Anhinga in some parts of the world are used with a harness to capture fish for the native people. A ring is placed around the neck to prevent the Anhinga from swallowing the fish, thereby providing food for its owner.

Anhinga

Great Blue Heron *Ardea herodias*

In wet areas along roadside ditches, lakes, streams, estuaries and coastal shorelines you can find the Great Blue Heron. The Great Blue Heron, Great Egret and Cattle Egret are the most common large wading birds found in Florida. The Cattle Egret and Great Egret are white, whereas the Great Blue Heron is a gray-blue. The Great Blue Heron stands around four feet in height with a wingspan of five to six feet.

The Great Blue Heron feeds upon any aquatic creature that it can catch while wading in shallow water. It is opportunistic in feeding but prefers fish as its staple food supply. Due to its close proximity to man the Heron has become quite adaptable to other food sources. At camp sites Herons take mice as well as a full-grown gray squirrels.

The Great Blue Heron is colonial in nesting, preferring from a few dozen to several hundred nests in groups called "rookeries." Most often the same nesting areas are used year after year. The nests are loosely constructed of sticks and leaves. These can be from ten to over fifty feet from the ground, the height depending on the vegetation available. In the south where tall trees are at a premium, nesting occurs in mangroves and willows. Three to four light blue-green eggs are laid in the nest beginning in November. Four weeks are needed to hatch with six to eight weeks to fledging, again dependant upon the food supply. Both parents incubate and feed the chicks. Predation of young is great while on the nests.

In the Keys and Florida Bay a White phase (White Morph) of the Great Blue Heron is found. This bird has a completely white body with yellow legs and yellow bill. The "Wurdemann's Heron" is supposed to be an intermediate bird between the two herons or possibly an offspring of mixed mating.

The Great Blue Heron is a great study in patience and stalking. Because its legs are quite long, the Blue Heron can wade and feed in relatively deep water. Sometimes this heron will be in water up to its body waiting for a fish or tadpole to swim by. If the fish is small it is usually swallowed on the spot, but occasionally I have seen these birds take a larger fish or snake to the shore where it will drop it and strike it repeatedly before swallowing it whole. As long as there is some success in capturing food the Heron will return to feed. This has caused major consternation with the many fish farms. The Great Blue Heron can also be a problem to the backyard pond enthusiast. The legal and most expedient way to stop the Herons from feeding is to place a network of lines, netting or some sort of protection over the pond.

Great Blue Heron

Great Egret   *Casmerodius albus*

The Great Egret and the Cattle Egret are probably the most recognizable of the birds that visitors see upon coming to Florida. These large, white birds are found along most waterways, ditches and lakes. Similar in size to the Great Blue Heron, the Great Egret is a completely white wading bird with a yellow bill which changes in color to bright-orange during breeding. It also has black legs and feet. Although the Great Egret is found quite extensively to the north, it is truly a Florida bird, being quite common except in the extreme northwest. During the winter an influx of northern migrants come into Florida.

Nesting occurs during the winter months; three eggs normally being laid. The nests are loose platforms of sticks and twigs with finer material lining the center. They are built in trees and shrubs from ten to fifty feet above the ground. The nests in the colonies sometimes number in the hundreds and they are often found mixed together with those of other wading birds. Most nests are built from ten to thirty feet apart.

The light-blue eggs take nearly four weeks to hatch and the young are fed regurgitated soft food at first, but soon begin to eat food left behind by the parents. The young are able to leave the nest at about four weeks. One brood of young is raised each year and the success of nesting is in-creasing with the ban of DDT and more environmental awareness. However, the Great Egret still has to compete with the loss of its habitat of wetlands.

Historically, the Great Egret, as well as some of the other egrets, were slaughtered for their beautiful breeding plumes. If you see these birds displaying during the breeding season you will understand the attraction for their exotic and exquisite plumes. Not much thought was given to collecting the birds during the mid-1800s and it is estimated that one-half million birds were killed. Today the Egret is the worldwide symbol of responsible conservation and preservation by the Audubon Society. It wasn't until the turn-of-the-century through concerted efforts that laws were passed and the use of plumes and feathers was no longer acceptable.

The Great Egret is a little more aggressive in its feeding habits than the Great Blue Heron. It will remain still and wait for its prey to swim or hop by, but it is also an aggressive stalker. Many times it will sneak up on a fish, frog or some aquatic prey and capture it in its long, pointed bill. Occasionally it will feed with other wading birds and even steal from nearby feeding birds such as ibis, storks and herons.

Great Egret

Cattle Egret *Bubulcus ibis*

This prolific and abundant white wading bird has an interesting history. The Cattle Egret is an import from Africa. The first Cattle Egret showed up in South America in the late 1800s and arrived in Florida and Texas by the middle of this century. The first breeding record occurred in the early 1950s. They have since expanded throughout the southern states. The migratory and wandering habits of this bird have made it show up in nearly every state east of the Mississippi. It has reached the west coast and is moving north from California.

In Africa, the Cattle Egret is known for following the antelope and other grazers of the savanna. As the land in Africa was taken over by farms and cattle, this bird began following cattle, hence the name Cattle Egret. The Cattle Egret is also known to sit on the backs of large animals such as the Cape buffalo, elephant and rhinoceros. In the United States it is known to ride the backs of livestock and even alligators. In agricultural areas, the Cattle Egret has adapted to following tractors tilling the soil searching for anything edible that might appear, from worms to mice.

This small egret is very common throughout the state, especially during the breeding season. During the winter the Cattle Egret flies even further south south so it is less abundant throughout Florida.

The breeding season is from March through the summer. Except during the breeding season, this small egret (18"-20") is all white with a yellow bill and yellowish-colored legs. In the breeding season the bird has rusty plumes on the head, back and lower neck. During breeding the legs become darker and the bill becomes bright-orange. This egret is a little more stocky and has shorter legs than other egrets. There is no place that this bird may not be found except in deeply-forested areas.

The Cattle Egret prefers to hunt in open areas, both dry and wet, where it seeks insects, small birds, mice, reptiles and amphibians. It normally takes advantage of other animals or humans to flush its prey.

The loose nest of reeds, sticks and twigs is placed in tall shrubs or small trees. Usually three or four light-blue eggs are laid in the nest and incubated by both sexes for just under four weeks. One adult broods the young for about three weeks. The young can leave the nest and be self-sufficient after a couple more weeks.

The Cattle Egret has become a suburban bird in some instances. An opportunist, the Cattle Egret will raid gardens and even dog bowls, although this behavior is not common enough to become a nuisance, probably because of the preference for a diet of living things.

Cattle Egret

Snowy Egret *Egretta thula*

This middle-sized Egret is most easily distinguished from the other egrets by the fact that it has bright-yellow feet and a black bill. The Snowy Egret's upper legs are black, which accentuates the black slipper-look of the feet. The bill has a yellow spot in front of the eye which turns bright-orange during the breeding season.

Another characteristic of the Snowy Egret which distinguishes it from other egrets is its active style of feeding. It rushes about seeking fish, frogs and other aquatic life. It is different from the white phase of the Reddish Egret, not only because it has yellow feet and a straight, black bill but because the Reddish Egret is usually a bit larger and spreads its wings when feeding. The immature white phase of the Little Blue Heron has yellow legs and a grey- to flesh-colored bill.

Like the other egrets, the Snowy Egret was hunted to near extinction for its plumes. The Snowy Egret has rebounded nicely, although in recent years their numbers seem to be declining. It is found throughout the state but can be common in one area and almost absent in others. During the winter, after migration, the northern part of Florida may be quite devoid of these birds.

The normal nesting season is from March through early summer but occasionally it may begin a little earlier. Nesting in colonies with other egrets and herons, the Snowy Egret places its nest of loosely-stacked sticks in trees and shrubs about ten to thirty feet above the ground. The male gathers the nesting material and the female builds the nest.

Three to five light blue-green eggs are laid in the nest and incubation begins with the first egg. This accounts for the hatching of eggs over a few days. Because of this staggered hatching, the youngest chicks may not survive during years of lean food supplies. The eggs take over three weeks to hatch and the young will be able to leave the nest about four weeks after hatching. Only one brood is produced each year.

During breeding, the Snowy Egret sports beautiful plumes of feathers as does the Great Egret. I believe the Snowy Egret is a much more striking bird during breeding season because of its jet-black legs and striking yellow feet. As in most of the egrets, the bill color changes dramatically during breeding and is quite remarkable.

The Snowy Egret also has the habit of following some of the more active wading birds, such as the Glossy Ibis and Reddish Egret, in order to take advantage of their active feeding and capture food stirred up by these birds.

Snowy Egret

Reddish Egret *Egretta rufescens*

The Reddish Egret is found throughout Florida and along the Gulf of Mexico coastline to Texas. Although not as common as the other egrets and wading birds the population has made enough of a comeback from the plume hunters to become common, especially near and along the coastline. One of the best sites to see this bird is the southern West Coast Island. The Reddish Egret can be found in southern Florida in most appropriate habitats, although it may not be numerous. During the non-breeding season this bird can be found in aquatic areas as far north as Alabama, Georgia, Louisiana and Texas.

Breeding may begin as early as December but normally begins after the first of the year and proceeds through late spring. Breeding plumes are present during the season along with blue patches in front of the eyes. The bills are flesh-colored except for a black tip. Both sexes build a platform of twigs in small shrubs and trees as well as mangroves.

Three or four light-blue eggs are laid and hatch in about four weeks. The young are fed regurgitated food; as they become older the pieces of food become larger. The young can leave the nest at about five weeks but will still be dependant upon the parents for as long as five more weeks.

The Reddish Egret gets its name from the reddish "mane" that the bird exhibits. Its body is gray with the bill flesh-colored except for the black tip. Its legs are blue-black in color. A white phase of the Reddish Egret is easily distinguished from the other white egrets by the leg and bill color. The Reddish Egret is about thirty inches tall, making it about medium in height among the egrets and herons.

Besides its color, the feeding habits of the Reddish Egret most distinguish it from other egrets. The Reddish Egret is one of the most aggressive wading birds in Florida. It spreads its wings and dashes back and forth pursuing fish and aquatic invertebrates. In a flock of birds feeding in the shallows of an estuary or lake edge, it is easy to pick out the Reddish Egret by its fits and starts as it darts to and fro chasing fish.

Some feel the Reddish Egret's spread wings give it the advantage of seeing its prey by cutting down glare from the sun while others propose that the shadow of the egret lures fish to a hiding place. The Reddish Egret may also be stirring up the bottom to chase out hidden prey. This egret is not adverse to taking advantage of prey stirred up by other wading birds, so you may find the Reddish Egret among flocks of ibis, storks and other herons and egrets.

Reddish Egret

Tricolored Heron *Egretta tricolor*

The Tricolored Heron was originally called the "Louisiana Heron." This medium-sized heron is just over two feet tall. The Tricolored Heron is easily distinguished from the other bluish-colored herons because of its size, blue head and zipper-like white stripe down the front of the neck. It has a white belly, while the Little Blue Heron is entirely blue. The Great Blue Heron has white on its head and a light-gray neck instead of blue. The Tricolored Heron has a yellow bill with black tip whereas the Little Blue Heron's bill is black or bluish. Although not extremely common, this bird can be found nearly anywhere in Florida in shallow wetland areas.

During the winter, local populations may be increased by migrants. Even though this bird was not as heavily sought after for its plumes the population is still not large today. As in all wetland dependant animals, the populations are being reduced by the loss of wetland habitats. The Tricolored Heron can be found along the Gulf Coast as far as Texas and along the Atlantic coast to the Carolinas.

As with all egrets and herons, the Tricolored Heron feeds on fish, frogs, aquatic invertebrates and anything else it can catch. This heron is good at stalking and may be aggressive in chasing schools of fish or tadpoles. You may see this heron walking across mats of water lettuce or water hyacinths as it searches for insects, frogs and crayfish.

A nest of loosely-arranged sticks is placed in shrubs and mangroves. Nesting begins in February and the nests are abandoned by spring. The nest is built by both parents and the three to four blue-green eggs are incubated by both parents for just over three weeks. The young are tended by both parents as well. As with most herons, the young are fed regurgitated food that is well-digested at first. As the chicks get older they begin to eat small pieces of fish until they can swallow small fish and insects entire.

The young are mature enough to leave the nest and fend for themselves at about five weeks. The immature birds have a russet-brown wash over the back and rump. The nests are usually found in colonies with the nests of other herons, egrets and ibis. Most often the nests are near saltwater and they do not occur with any regularity in the interior of the state.

Immature birds and migrating birds can become quite the wanderers north of their normal coastal range however, their affinity for saltwater will probably limit the populations to the coastlines of the United States. As in many parts of Florida the elimination of wetlands will be a dramatic factor in population numbers and growth.

Tricolored Heron

Little Blue Heron   *Egretta caerulea*

Another medium-sized heron, the Little Blue Heron is all blue in color and about two feet in height. Unlike the other blue-colored herons, the Little Blue Heron is entirely blue while other blue herons have some white on them. The bill of this heron is dark with a black tip. In all plumages, except the immature, there is no white on the Little Blue Heron. The immature bird is white but has the dark bill. In breeding plumage, the neck feathers change from a slate-blue to a reddish- to maroon-blue and the legs become black instead of yellow-green. The immature white birds become mottled as the white feathers are replaced with blue feathers during the first year, making it easy to identify them.

Although not sought out for its plumes, the population of these birds has been declining because of habitat loss and possible competition of nesting sites with the introduced Cattle Egret. The Little Blue Heron seems to compliment the Tricolored Heron by preferring the freshwaters and interior of Florida, although they can be found throughout the state.

The feeding habits of the Little Blue Heron are closer to that of the Great Blue Heron and Green-Backed Heron than the other herons and egrets. The Little Blue Heron is a deliberate stalker, but is quite slow, often remaining in one spot to capture prey as it passes by. The Little Blue Heron, Great Blue Heron and Green-Backed Heron three are masters at standing perfectly still, allowing the prey to approach the "large grey stump"—whereupon they become a meal. The herons exhibit amazing stealth and stretching ability. It sometimes seems that the heron will fall over as it s-t-r-e-t-c-h-e-s to spear a fish or unwary frog. They seem to know just the distance needed to strike and be successful.

Nesting begins in February when both sexes build a loose platform of sticks in which three or four bluish-green eggs are laid. The nests are found in colonies with those of other herons and egrets. The eggs hatch in about three-and-a-half weeks and the young leave the nest in six to seven weeks. The male bird protects the nest during incubation, even if he is unable to feed during this time. The nest is brooded about half the time in rearing, but as the young are able to maintain their body temperature and withstand the weather, the brooding stops except in harsh weather.

The Little Blue Heron can be found in many of the sanctuaries and wetlands, both on the coast as well as the interior of the state. Corkscrew Sanctuary as well as Everglades National Park are two good areas to view this quite beautiful bird.

Little Blue Heron

Green-backed Heron   *Butorides striatus*

This smallest heron is only a foot-and-a-half tall, and is one of most secretive. Preferring to remain hidden, the Green-backed Heron habituates wooded swamplands throughout Florida and much of the United States. Not as colonial as some of the other herons the Green-backed Heron (formerly called the "Green Heron") normally feeds solitarily. It can be found throughout Florida in wetlands.

The Green-backed Heron is a small, chubby bird with an iridescent-green back. Its legs are yellow-green; the male's legs become bright-orange during breeding season. The cape, or neck, is russet-colored with a white stripe running down the neck similar to the Tricolored Heron. The undersides are white with an iridescent green-black crown sometimes raised in a crest, in which the feathers stand straight up.

The Green-backed Heron is the most solitary and sedate of the herons in feeding, infrequently pursuing its prey. Its usual method of obtaining food is to sit on a log, branch or just along the bank waiting for a fish, frog or some small crustacean. It may remain motionless for long periods of time while waiting for just the correct moment. When the fish is within striking distance the heron will lash out its long neck and pierce the fish with its bill. If the fish is small it will flip it to swallow it headfirst. If the fish is large, it may wade ashore and position it in order to swallow it. The larger bill of this heron allows it to catch larger prey.

Nesting begins in March and is completed by June. Most often, the Green-backed Heron is a solitary nester in trees and shrubs of about thirty feet. In suburban areas, it likes to nest in clumps of coniferous trees. Occasionally it will nest with others of its species, even more rarely it nests with other herons, ibis or egrets. A platform of intertwined twigs and sticks is created and holds about four bluish-green eggs. If at all possible, the nest will be near water, even overhanging the water. In recent years, this tendency has been somewhat reduced probably due to lack of nesting sites.

The eggs hatch in about three-and-a-half weeks and the young will leave in another four weeks. Before leaving the nest the young climb about the nest and tree with ease. The young cannot take care of themselves for another month, and are therefore attended to by the adults until the youngsters learn to forage for themselves.

Green-backed Heron

Black- and Yellow-crowned Night-heron

Nycticorax nycticorax and Nyctanassa violacea

These two herons are among the most interesting of the wading birds found in Florida. Probably the most interesting feature of these birds is, as their name indicates, their habit of feeding extensively during the night, unlike the other herons and egrets. The Night-herons have larger bills for their size and so are able to take advantage of larger prey.

Identifying these birds is relatively easy. They are both over two feet tall, rather chunky, and when seen during the day are usually roosting. The immature birds are brown with spots on the back and streaks on the front. It is difficult to distinguish the two types of young Night-herons from each other, but the adult birds are easier to differentiate. Both of the Night-herons are gray overall. The Black-crowned Heron has a black crown and a black back. The Yellow-crowned Heron lacks the black back and has the yellow crown and a black chin that extends to the back of the head, producing the effect of a white patch behind the eye on the cheek.

The necks of the Night-herons are not as long as other herons, possibly because their night-hunting habits make it less necessary to get as close to their prey. Both Night-herons have plumes which arise from the head during breeding season. The legs of the adults are yellow or yellow-green except during breeding. Of the two, the Black-crowned is most likely to be seen. The Yellow-crowned is more secretive and may not be as abundant. Adult plumage is not obtained in both species until the third year.

The Night-herons feed on the same prey as the other herons but not necessarily the same species. Feeding at night, they are inclined to be more opportunistic, taking just about anything living they come across. This may include small mammals, birds and a whole host of amphibians. The main diet, of course, is fish and aquatic invertebrates.

The Night-herons can be found throughout the state and are increasingly abundant as the winter migrants return. The preferred habitat is shrubby, wooded shorelines where they can creep and feed along near the water's edge. If they feed during the day, they will wade in shallow water especially near mangroves.

Their eggs are a light blue-green and are laid in a loose platform of sticks and twigs. Their nests are more securely hidden than those of the other herons. The eggs hatch after about three weeks and the adults feed the young partially digested to small undigested food. Feeding occurs at dawn, dusk and throughout the night.

These birds are quite striking and you can see them readily if you look in trees, mangroves and shrubs in wet areas. In populated areas, they may forage during the day along with other herons.

Black-crowned Night-heron (bottom)
Yellow-crowned Night-heron (top)

American Bittern *Botaurus lentiginosus*

The America Bittern is one of the hardest of the heron group to locate, not only because of its low numbers but because it is extremely well camouflaged. Being just a little taller than the night-herons, the American Bittern is all brown with a buff-colored belly and front. A dark brown-to-black streak arises from the bill and goes down the neck to the shoulder. In flight the American Bittern shows black wingtips with a brown back. This bird has broken streaks running down the entire front. The brown back is somewhat mottled.

When disturbed or when trying to conceal itself the American Bittern will point its long bill skyward and blend in perfectly with the cattails or the marsh grass it frequents. The American Bittern is so adept at this that its eyes are able to look straight forward even when its bill points skyward. The young on the nest also have this ability and when frightened will become a cluster of cattails with their eyes looking straight at you!

The American Bittern can be found in marshes throughout the state of Florida, becoming more abundant during the winter when migrants from around the eastern United States arrive. This bird is relatively common but some discussion exists as to whether it breeds in the state any longer. The Bittern has not adapted well to man and is extremely sensitive to the loss of marshlands, its prime habitat.

The American Bittern is a master of stealth. Coupled with its extremely well-camouflaged body it is very adept at capturing food in the marsh. Its primary foods are amphibians, fish, numerous invertebrates, crayfish, small mammals and even small birds You might say the Bittern is an opportunist.

Nesting occurs from April to June in the heavy grasses of marshlands. The nest may be on land, in dense marsh grasses or in cattails. The nest is constructed of larger pieces of sticks and marsh vegetation made into a mat. Four or five buff-colored eggs are laid and are incubated for about four weeks. The young are fed regurgitated food and grow very quickly. At about two weeks the young leave the nest, blending well with the marsh vegetation. The young may follow the parents for a time.

A common name for the American Bittern is "Thunder Pump," apparently because of the deep calls the male makes during courtship. In the marshes, during the night, they make a deep resonant *kunk-a-lunk* which is repeated four or five times. This call is most common during the predawn hours. Once you have heard this call it will remain with you and bring a smile to your face as you recognize the origin.

American Bittern

Wood Stork   *Mycteria americana*

Standing about three-and-a-half feet tall, the Wood Stork is easily recognized and frequently sought by amateur birders. This bird is primarily white with black wingtips and black tail. The head is featherless and gray and its legs are black with pink feet, which differs from the yellow stockings of the Snowy Egret. In flight, the black wingtips and black tail are pronounced. Its bill is long and curves gently down at the tip. The immature birds sport a yellow bill while in the adults it is dark gray.

Shallow concentrated water is prime habitat for the Wood Stork because of the way it captures its prey. It places its bill in the water and slowly moves about with the bill open. The movement of the bird and stirring of the feet cause aquatic organisms and fish to become frightened and seek safety. What better place to hide than this narrow space between two sticks in the water? The Wood Stork's bill is extremely sensitive and as soon as a fish enters the space between the bill it snaps shut. Sight is not a prerequisite for feeding. Because of this feeding habit, the Wood Stork prefers shallow pools from the dry season to concentrate the fish. It is not extremely successful during rainy seasons or, of course, if there is a drought.

Although not as common as they once were, the Wood Storks can be easily seen in the right habitat. Corkscrew Sanctuary is one of the most reliable places to see these birds. The Wood Stork breeds in Florida, although not in the panhandle and extreme northern portions of the state. Post-breeding season sees the birds dispersing over the southeast and even traveling as far north as the Carolinas and Tennessee.

A very colonial nester, the Wood Stork prefers the mangroves and cypress swamps. As many as two dozen nests may be placed in a cypress tree on large branches that are parallel to the ground. A fairly loose nest of sticks is made and lined with softer plant materials and green leaves. Usually three white eggs are laid as early as November and may last until the next spring. Nesting is determined by the availability of food. If the water is high, nesting will not occur and even if nesting is begun and heavy rains occur, nests may be abandoned.

The eggs hatch in about four weeks and the young will fledge in about eight weeks. Breeding birds are more than three years old. Until the correlation between water level and nesting was discovered much consternation was expressed when the Wood Stork would not nest. Today the bird is heavily studied but scientists are more at ease. If you wish to see these birds it is easiest during nesting when they are concentrated and feeding their young.

Wood Stork

Roseate Spoonbill *Ajaia ajaja*

Probably no large wading bird causes such excitement as does the Roseate Spoonbill. From the beginner the first thing you hear is, "Look, a Flamingo!" This large, pink bird is easily seen from a distance and Florida is synonymous with Flamingos, so of course, that's what it has to be. But Wild Flamingos are extremely rare in Florida, so most often we are looking at the beautiful Roseate Spoonbill.

At just under three feet tall, the Roseate Spoonbill is easily identified. The adults are pink in color with a bright-orange tail and bright-pink accents on the upper wings and rump. The other common bird that may be confused with the Spoonbill is the Scarlet Ibis, although the Scarlet Ibis is a uniform pink over its entire body, including the legs. The neck and upper back of the spoonbill are white. The Spoonbill's head is featherless except for on immature birds. The most striking feature is the long, flat bill, spoon-shaped at the end—hence the name Spoonbill. Immature birds are predominately white, turning to the adult pink over two to three years.

These birds can commonly be seen wading in shallow water sweeping their spoon-shaped bill back and forth, feeding on aquatic organisms. They are most common in the southern part of Florida and along the coasts. After breeding, the birds may disperse all along the Gulf coast, even as far as Texas. You may also find wandering birds up the Atlantic coastline. Breeding populations may be augmented by strays from Texas and Mexico as individuals may move along the Gulf of Mexico coastline.

Nesting may begin as early as November in the southern part of Florida but not until April in the north. Usually three white eggs are laid in a very deep nest in shrubs about twenty feet above the ground. Often the nests are in mixed colonies with egrets, herons and ibis. The male usually brings the nesting material to the female who then builds the nest. This nest is probably the best built of the large wading birds. The eggs hatch in just over three weeks and the babies may take from five to six weeks before leaving the nest. The young are fed regurgitated food from the parents and are able to move about the nest and tree in a few weeks, just before leaving the nest.

Although the populations have rebounded from the use of their feathers in hats and fans, there is still concern over these birds. The loss of habitat, especially shallow water, has shifted and even eliminated some populations. Draining of wetlands must be regulated and large expanses of wetlands must be preserved for these and many of Florida's wetland species.

Roseate Spoonbill

Greater Flamingo *Phoenicopterus ruber*

If you ask any child or adult what bird they wish to see in Florida, it will undoubtedly be the Flamingo or the Pelican. In fact, the Flamingo is almost synonymous with Florida largely due to the extremely effective ad campaigns of Busch Gardens, Disney World and many other tourist attractions. Even though these birds can be from wild populations, most of us will see the Greater Flamingo in flocks that have an ancestry from zoos or theme parks.

The Greater Flamingo prefers to feed in shallow, saline water where it sweeps its head back and forth sifting for crustaceans, shrimp and other aquatic organisms. Except for the resident flocks of birds it is a rare migrant from Cuba, the Caribbean, the Bahamas and Mexico. The migrant birds are found only in extreme southern parts of Florida. Except for resident escaped flocks, you will only see the Flamingo during the winter months. In other parts of the tropical world, the Flamingo exists in the hundreds of thousands and can be a truly remarkable sight wading about a shallow lake or in flight.

The Flamingo is about the size of the Great Blue Heron, being around four feet tall. It is a bright-pink color overall with pink legs. The large bill is turned down and is black at the end. When in flight the Flamingo is not difficult to identify. The neck stretches out in front of the bird and the legs hang straight out in back. It almost appears symmetrical. The large pink bird shows a lot of black in the trailing edges of the wings. Birds from captive flocks are generally not as bright-pink as wild birds.

When in flight or on the ground they may give a goose-like call which is, however, somewhat more nasal in quality. Because it is easy to confuse the Flamingo and the Roseate Spoonbill, a look at their bills and legs will make it obvious which is which. The Spoonbill is also much smaller than the Flamingo. Another all pink bird that is sometimes confused with the Flamingo is the Scarlet Ibis. However, this bird is much smaller with a long, slender, down-curved bill.

There is some discussion about whether these birds ever nested in Florida. The consensus is that probably they did not. There is some speculation about whether some captive flocks are breeding without aid in Florida today, but it is not agreed on whether to classify these birds as wild or escapees.

One blue-green egg is laid in a raised mud mound in a shallow lake. After about a four week incubation period the egg hatches. The young leave the nest to forage with the adults in about a week. The young and immature birds are a dirty white in color, not the bright-pink of the adults.

Greater Flamingo

White Ibis *Eudocimus albus*

Although many do not realize it, this white wading bird is probably one of the most numerous of its color in the southern part of Florida with the possible exception of the Cattle Egret. The White Ibis may be found throughout Florida in marshes, lakes, streams and other wetlands. Occasionally they may be found feeding in pastures and fields. The White Ibis is also common along the entire Gulf Coast and the Atlantic Coast to the Carolinas. After breeding season individuals may spread northward as far as the Great Lakes. It wasn't until recent years that the White Ibis was found to breed in northern Florida and the panhandle.

The White Ibis prefers to feed in freshwater marshes, shallow streams and lakes as well as estuaries. They prefer salt marshes to fresher water. The favorite diet of the White Ibis consists of a whole variety of crustaceans, including crabs, shrimp and crayfish. A major part of their diet also includes fish, snakes, insects and many small mollusks. As with most of the wading birds, they are opportunists and will take anything that is easily captured and swallowed.

The two-foot tall White Ibis is easily differentiated from the other white wading birds by a couple of characteristics. The adult White Ibis has a red face and bill except for the black tip. The legs of adults are red. The bill is long and curves downward in the typical ibis shape. Immature birds are dark above with a white belly. In flight, the White Ibis flies in typical "V" formation or in a straight line. Because of the large number of birds in a flock, these formations may extend for over a mile in length. The tips of the white wings are black but the black area is not very extensive. Occasionally you will see a light-pink ibis that is probably a hybrid between the White Ibis and the pink Scarlet Ibis.

The White Ibis is extremely colonial and nests in dense colonies numbering into the thousands. The nests are rather substantial and are found in shorter trees and shrubs. Material is added to the nest as the nesting season progresses. Nesting begins in March and extends into mid-spring.

Two to three light blue-green eggs marked with various darker colors are incubated for about three weeks. The young are fed regurgitated food and are able to leave the nest in about five weeks. The young will usually follow the main flocks as they go from one feeding area to another.

Although the populations of White Ibis are not endangered, they are declining because of the loss of wetlands and areas for nesting.

White Ibis

Glossy Ibis *Plegadis falcinellus*

Increasing in population as well as territory, the Glossy Ibis can be found throughout Florida, primarily in freshwater marshes and wetlands. Since the middle of this century the populations have increased dramatically. The populations are expanding along the Gulf Coast to Texas and the Atlantic coast to Virginia, although stragglers may be found as far north as the Great Lakes and along the Atlantic into Canada.

Standing about two feet tall, the Glossy Ibis, from a distance, appears dark, almost black. Upon a closer look, the Glossy Ibis shows how it got its name. The body of the Glossy Ibis is a deep-maroon to chestnut color and their wings are a deep-green color. The feathers appear to have a metallic sheen hence the name "Glossy Ibis." The bill is a dark-olive color and the legs are dark-green with maroon joints. In the right light and from a distance, the Glossy Ibis may appear to be deep maroon-red to dark-pink. The long, decurved "ibis" bill is typical.

In flight, the Glossy Ibis, like the White Ibis, flies in a long or "V"-shaped line. The flocks of Glossy Ibis are not as extensive as the White Ibis. In flight, the Glossy Ibis is entirely dark with its head and neck extended and legs trailing.

The Glossy Ibis feeds extensively with other ibis, herons and egrets.

Like the White Ibis, the diet of the Glossy Ibis consists of crabs, crayfish, mollusks, insects, snakes and crustaceans. In freshwater, where it seems to prevail, their main diet is crayfish.

The preferred nesting area of the Glossy Ibis is wooded swamps and marshes where it will nest in small trees or shrubs. The nest is fairly substantial and becomes more so as the brooding occurs as new material is added while incubating and during rearing of the young.

Two to four blue-green eggs are laid in the nest in May and hatching occurs after three weeks of incubation. The female does the honors at night but both will incubate during the day. About four weeks are needed for the chicks to be able to leave the nest. The parents regurgitate food directly to the young for the first few weeks, but thereafter they eat food left at the nest side. The young will take up to seven weeks to leave the nest after which they will forage with their parents. The young hatch in the order in which the eggs are laid, so the earlier, stronger young will be assured of survival during the sometimes tenuous summertime feeding. By the end of July most of the nests have been abandoned. Some feel that this staggering of nesting times with the White Ibis may be done so as not to be in competition for the same food supply for young at the nest.

Glossy Ibis

Fulvous Whistling Duck   *Dendrocygna bicolor*

Known as a rare vagrant until the 1950s, the Fulvous Whistling Duck has literally exploded in population in southern Florida, especially near Lake Okeechobee. New populations are being discovered in isolated areas throughout the state, except in the panhandle. These ducks have adapted extremely well to agricultural areas in Florida, especially the rice fields. Juvenile birds are apparently afflicted with a wanderlust and appear in the states bordering Florida and occasionally further north. The original populations may have been descendants of wild flocks that happened to visit Florida or they may be from captive flocks in botanic gardens and theme parks. The adaptation to the world of man has allowed this duck to become prolific in city parks, theme parks and any public wetlands.

Probably more closely related to swans and geese than true ducks, the Fulvous Whistling Duck is quite striking. It is a rather slender duck standing quite tall while on the ground. The overall color is a rich fawn-brown with a dark-brown to black back. The back feathers are scalloped in the same fawn color on the edges, giving a fish scale pattern to the back. The lower throat has a light area with streaking before a solid fawn color takes over again. A black stripe runs down the back of the neck from the top of the head down to the shoulder.

The legs and bill are a dark gray in color. This bird breeds in Texas but the populations there are declining.

The Fulvous Whistling Duck is primarily a vegetarian, feeding upon algae, rice and seeds in shallow waterways. This duck feeds mostly during the nighttime hours. Occasionally it will take small insects, crustaceans and snails. It has adapted well to the backwater flood plains of Florida's rivers.

The Fulvous Whistling Duck nests during the summer months in a nest made of grasses and other vegetation and lined with finer grasses. The nest may be on dry ground between or next to marshes. The nest may also be placed on a mound of vegetation built up in the middle of a marsh. About a dozen white eggs are laid in the nest over a couple weeks. Since the female may lay up to five dozen eggs she may "dump" some of her eggs in another duck's nest.

The male and female form a long-term bond, perhaps even a mating for life, much like the Canada Goose. Both take care of incubating and caring for the young. Eggs hatch in about three-and-a-half weeks, unlike many ducks and geese which take longer. After a day of drying, the young ducks follow the parents into the water and remain dependant for another couple months.

Fulvous Whistling Duck

Wood Duck *Aix sponsa*

The Wood Duck is absolutely the most beautiful of Florida's waterfowl. This small duck can be found throughout the wooded wetlands of Florida where it nests and feeds. The male is the most brightly-colored of the two sexes. Both sexes have a swept back crest, somewhat reminiscent of the hair styles of young men in the 1960s. The male's head is an iridescent-green with white stripes running through it. The bill is bright-orange or red at the base and matches the red eyes. The throat is bright-white which accents the green head. The side is buff-colored and outlined with darker upper body parts. The mahogany-speckled breast is gorgeous, with a broad, white stripe that separates it from the buff-colored side. The female is a more drab brown with lighter underparts. She has a white eye-ring which extends to make an eye-stripe which flows backward. Both have light-blue speculum on the wings which are evident when in flight.

During the winter the resident population is augmented with migrants from the rest of the United States. Populations at mid-century were extremely low due to hunting and loss of woodland wetlands. Today, with emphasis on habitat, better hunting controls and concerted conservation efforts the populations of this fantastic duck have rebounded significantly.

The Wood Duck is a tree-cavity nester and the loss of wooded swamps have taken away the nesting trees required for this bird's successful nesting. Nesting begins in February. The female lays an egg a day until twelve to twenty eggs are laid. Upon completing her clutch, she then incubates the eggs for about four weeks.

After hatching, the female allows the ducklings to dry for about twenty-four hours after which she leaves the nest in the tree and goes to the ground. She begins calling them, whereupon the ducklings climb up the inside of the tree cavity with their claw-like feet and jump to the ground. The height may be as much as forty feet, but this doesn't seem to deter or harm the ducklings. Once all the ducklings are gathered, the female will lead them to water where they will be more protected from predators. They will stay together as a family group for about two months. The male does not help with family duties after the eggs are hatched. Young ducklings imprint on the female and will keep running until they find her or die, making it very difficult for humans to raise young Wood Ducks. Two broods a year may be raised in the south, but only one in the north.

Wood Ducks eat aquatic plants, insects, crustaceans, berries, grain products and acorns. In some localities acorns are the predominant food.

Wood Duck
Female (top)   Male (bottom)

Mallard   *Anas platyrhynchos*

Normally considered a duck of the north, the Mallard is found throughout Florida, especially during the winter months as northern migrating birds invade the state. Although not considered a breeding bird in Florida, you may find some ponds and waterways with breeding Mallards. These are probably domesticated birds. You will find wild Mallards in Florida during the months of September through March. The greatest influx of birds comes after the waters of the north have frozen solid in November and December.

Most Mallards return north just as the ice leaves the lakes and streams to lay eggs and produce a single brood of ducklings. Each year the number of Mallards spending the winter in Florida is different. Influencing the numbers is the spring hatch, hunting pressure along the migration route and the severity of the winter, both timing and temperature. The extreme southern parts of Florida receive the least number of Mallards.

Identifying the Mallard is relatively easy. The male is also called a "Green Head" because he has a head that is entirely green. The bill is yellow or greenish-yellow and the green is bordered by a band of white. It is the only duck with these characteristics. The Northern Shoveler has a green head but the bill is different and the neck band is absent. If the head were not striking enough, the male has a bright-mahogany colored breast with gray feathers on its sides. The tail is black-and-white with a few curled feathers on the top. The back is light-brown. The female is not nearly as colorful, being predominately mottled brown with an orange-yellow bill with some black on it. Both sexes have orange feet and a bright-blue speculum that is bordered on top and bottom with a white stripe. This bright-blue area is most evident in flight with a little showing as they sit or swim.

In extreme southern Florida, the Mottled Duck, although rare, may be confused with the female Mallard. The main distinguishing feature of the Mottled Duck is the yellow bill which has no other markings.

The Mallard is a dabbling duck; it remains on the surface of the water to do the bulk of its feeding. The Mallard will sift through the shallow water with its head under water. It feeds mainly upon aquatic vegetation, small invertebrates and crustaceans. In deeper water it will "tip up" with its entire front body under water while it sifts through the bottom vegetation. In agricultural lands it has adapted well to grain products of all types.

During the winter months the female does the mate selection for the most part and returns to the area in which she was reared, taking her selected mate with her.

Mallard
Female (top)   Male (bottom)

Blue-winged Teal   *Anas discors*

One of the smallest ducks to visit the state of Florida is the Blue-winged Teal. This small duck is probably also the most abundant of the winter visitors. The Blue-winged Teal is also the migrating duck that spends the most time in Florida—from late July into the following May. Most birds arrive in early fall and leave by late March of the following year. This little duck can be found throughout Florida where there is shallow water allowing it to feed. During migration it can be found in most any body of water.

Besides its small size, the Blue-winged Teal is quite easy to identify. The male has a gray head, black forehead and prominent white moon-shaped crescent in front of the eye which follows the front of the head from top to bottom. The forehead is a darker gray. The body of both the male and female is brown with mottles or specks of black. Both have bright-green speculum with sky-blue wing patches from the speculum to the forewing, which are noticeable in flight. The male Blue-winged Teal has a black rear with a prominent white spot on the lower body in front of the black area.

Nesting is erratic in Florida as in many southern states. The female builds a nest in grass in order to hide it. The nest is constructed not far from water with whatever plant materials are available: usually grasses, sedges and cattails.

After a clutch of about twelve to fifteen cream-colored eggs is laid, down from the hen is added to the nest. Incubation lasts just short of four weeks. About a day after the ducklings dry, the hen will lead them to water where food and protection is more readily available. The ducklings remain with the hen until they begin to fly and may even migrate with the hen in family groups. The male abandons the female after the eggs begin to hatch and goes through a molt whereupon it resembles the immature and female birds until well into the fall.

One of the dabbling ducks, the Blue-winged Teal feeds in shallow water, preferring freshwater. The Blue-winged Teal feeds on aquatic vegetation from the surface and the soft bottom mud, rarely diving below the water with its entire body. Most of its food consists of seeds and small aquatic plants, but the Blue-winged Teal will also take small aquatic insects, crustaceans and snails. Both agricultural and natural seeds are also an important part of the diet of this small duck. After the harvest season, you may see numerous birds landing in fields to glean spilled corn, oats, rice or any grain.

Blue-winged Teal
Female (bottom)   Male (top)

Hooded Merganser *Lophodytes cucullatus*

A cavity nester like the Wood Duck, the Hooded Merganser has a crest or a hood. Although not as brilliantly colored as the Wood Duck, the Hooded Merganser is quite striking. The crest of the male has a black upper body and a yellow eye. The male's has a bright-white, fan-shaped patch in it. When the male does his courtship display, the crest is opened and the white patch is almost a quarter circle. When the Merganser is at rest or feeding, the white in the crest may appear as a white streak, sometimes almost absent. The breast of the male is white with black streaks on a diagonal from back to belly. Some white also shows in the wing. The side or flank of the male is a rich-brown which accentuates the black back. Both sexes have white wing patches in flight.

The female is a light chocolate-brown all over with a darker head. It is easily recognized as a merganser by the small, pointed bill and fan-shaped crest. The reddish-brown hood of the female is more wispy at the edges, appearing almost unkempt. The female Merganser is rather small, being only a foot-and-a-half long.

Predominately a winter resident of Florida, the Hooded Merganser has become a nesting species of the state. Common in winter on freshwater ponds and lakes, the Hooded Merganser is rare in the extreme southern parts of Florida and the Keys. Although it can be found in almost any body of water, it prefers wooded swamps and freshwater streams where it seeks out trees it needs for nesting.

Sharing the same nest cavities as Wood Ducks, the Hooded Merganser will even "dump" eggs in the nest of a Wood Duck. This, of course, will cause a mixed brood to be raised. Since the Hooded Merganser dumps eggs in other duck's nests the clutch of eggs can become quite large, sometimes numbering over thirty. In such a large clutch the hen is not able to incubate them all successfully, but clutches of twenty can be successful.

The normal clutch of eggs is about a dozen and takes about four-and-a-half weeks to hatch. As in the Wood Ducks the hen will allow the ducklings to dry and then lead them from the nest to water. The ducklings are able to fend for themselves upon achieving flight but may stay together as a family group for a considerable time. Successful nesting will lead to reuse of the same nest cavity or nest box. Wood Duck boxes have helped the populations of these birds and may be one factor for their increasing nesting in Florida.

Like most of the Mergansers, the Hooded Merganser is a fish eater with its pointed, saw-edged bill. It may feed upon any animal with which in comes in contact.

Hooded Merganser
Female (back)   Male (front)

Ruddy Duck *Oxyura jamaicensis*

A common winter resident of Florida in lakes, ponds, estuaries, fresh and salt marshes and even the ocean, the Ruddy Duck is one of the smallest of the diving ducks in the state. This short, squat duck is only a couple of inches over a foot long. The male in breeding plumage is quite striking. The body is a rich red-brown throughout. The head sports a large, white cheek patch with the top being black and the bill bright-blue. The black tail is normally fanned out and stands straight up, hence the nickname "stiff-tail" or "spike-tail."

During the winter the male is colored much like the female, a gray-brown with a white cheek patch and the bill a dull blue-gray. The female is distinguished from the male during the winter by a dark line across the white cheek patch. Both sexes have large heads and wide bills in proportion to their body. These characteristic features make it easy to identify this little duck even from a distance. Even without seeing its distinct features, the silhouette makes it unmistakable.

Even though it is considered a diving duck, and diving ducks are usually fish eaters, the primary diet of the Ruddy Duck is small aquatic invertebrates such as insects and crustaceans. In the winter it will take snails and some aquatic vegetation. The Ruddy Duck feeds by completely submerging or diving down to the bottom and gleaning from vegetation. It strains the bottom mud much like a Mallard does. The large bill makes this duck very efficient at obtaining food from the soft bottoms of marshes and lakes.

The Ruddy Duck spends the winters in Florida as well as much of the south, from the central Atlantic coast to Mexico and Central America. In recent years, the Ruddy Duck has been found nesting in parts of north Florida. The normal nesting area of the Ruddy Duck is the Central Plains and, increasingly, the Great Lakes area.

The Ruddy Duck is not comfortable on land so it usually nests near water in dense marsh vegetation. The nest is constructed from the vegetation at hand and lined with finer grasses and plant materials. About eight creamy-white eggs are a normal clutch and are incubated for about two-and-a-half weeks. After the young are dry they are able to follow the hen and can begin diving for food in a short time. This diving ability also allows them to escape predators quickly. The young begin to fend for themselves after a couple of months although northern broods may remain together as a family into migration. Nesting in Florida occurs during the summer months, coinciding with the nesting to the north.

Ruddy Duck
Female (top)   Male (bottom)

Black Vulture and Turkey Vulture

Coragyps atratus and Cathartes aura

These two vultures are the most common vultures in North America. The Black Vulture and Turkey Vulture are both large and black with the Black Vulture being the smaller of the two. With their wingspan of five or six feet, these birds are often mistaken for eagles because of their size. Vultures have small heads which are devoid of feathers—which most likely helps keep their head clean when they feed on rotting carcasses. The material from the carcasses dries up and falls off the bare skin of the head and upper neck.

The Vulture's bill is sharply hooked (as in many raptors) but instead of using its bill to capture prey it is used to tear apart the decaying bodies of its prey. Vultures have a good sense of smell, unusual for many birds, which helps them locate carrion from great distances. The Black Vulture has a less sensitive sense of smell than the Turkey Vulture. Road kills have become a significant part of these two vultures' diet.

These two vultures are relatively easy to tell apart. The head of the adult Turkey Vulture is red in color, whereas the Black Vulture's is a dark-gray. The immature Turkey Vulture is also gray. In soaring flight, the Turkey Vulture keeps its wings at an angle to its body making it appear like the letter "V" from the ground. The Turkey Vulture also tips from side to side in flight so the "V" is quite evident. The Black Vulture keeps its wings parallel to the ground, presenting a straight line from wingtip to wingtip. Since both Vultures have small heads, the flight silhouette appears almost headless. In flight, the tail of the Black Vulture is very short and squared off at the end. Its legs stretch back to the end of the tail and, in some cases, may extend beyond the tail. This characteristics is never true in the case of the Turkey Vulture.

The wing patterns are also used to differentiate these two birds. The Black Vulture's shorter wings have white patches at the ends, whereas the Turkey Vulture has light patterns in the entire trailing edge of the wings from primaries to the body. Both species are more prevalent during the winter with the influx of individuals from the north. The Turkey Vulture is the most common.

Both vultures are communal in their roosting habits and you may find whole trees full of these birds in the early morning before the warm air thermals take them away to feed. These birds can be found anywhere in Florida.

Black Vulture and Turkey Vulture
Turkey Vulture, in flight (second from top, in flight and full picture)
Black Vulture, in flight (top) and Head (left center)

Bald Eagle *Haliaeetus leucocephalus*

Florida has the largest breeding population of Bald Eagles outside Alaska in the United States. This symbol of our heritage can be found throughout Florida wherever it can obtain food and can remain relatively undisturbed. The Bald Eagle has come under extreme pressure over much of the United States because of pesticides and loss of habitat. With the banning of DDT and concerted efforts to maintain good breeding habitats, especially in the north, the Bald Eagle is holding its own and even making a comeback in some areas.

The largest of our raptors, or birds of prey, the Bald Eagle is easy to identify. The adult eagle has an all-white head and tail which is evident in flight or at rest. The large, hooked bill is bright-yellow, as is the feet. The eagle stands over three feet tall and has a wingspan of six to seven feet. The immature Bald Eagle does not sport the white head and tail until after three to five years, most often in four years. You can distinguish the eagle from a Turkey Vulture by the flat wing pattern of the eagle when in flight as compared to the V-shaped form of the Turkey Vulture's wings. Immature eagles have been known to attempt mating and building nests in the proper habitats before reaching mature plumage.

The Bald Eagle is primarily a fish eater, catching fish near the surface by flying low over the water and grasping them in its powerful talons. Although preferring fish, they are not adverse to taking anything which might be available such as muskrat, ducks or any water bird. The Bald Eagle has also been known to steal fish and food from other predators, especially the Osprey. The Bald Eagle is also known to be a carrion eater, especially along northern rivers during the winter and in times of stress. During the winter, northern Florida may receive an influx of these birds.

In Florida, the Bald Eagle nests in tall trees, primarily conifers. The nest is extremely large and is normally used year after year, being added to each year. Some nests are estimated to weigh more than a ton. The courtship of the Bald Eagle is quite spectacular. The mated pair locks their bright-yellow talons and descend downward in a large spiral performing flips or somersaults. This may be repeated several times. Nesting begins in early winter and a normal clutch is two bluish-white eggs. The eggs hatch in five weeks and the young are attended by both parents. Since the young may hatch a couple of days apart, if food is at a premium most often the youngest will perish. It will take about two months for the young eagles to be able to fly and leave the nest.

Bald Eagle

Mississippi Kite and Snail Kite

Ictinia mississippiensis and Rostrhamus sociabilis

Kites are birds of prey that are markedly different from the other raptors. The kites are normally found in the southern parts of the United States. The Snail Kite is found only in Florida and can usually be found along the Tamiami Trail, Alligator Alley and in the Big Cypress National Preserve.

The Mississippi Kite is a striking bird about fifteen inches tall. The male is a dark-gray on the upper body parts and tail while the breast, belly and head are light-gray. The eye is a bright orange-red. The immature birds are heavily streaked on the breast and the upper gray is mottled. In the air, except at close range, the Mississippi Kite appears similar to a large, dark swallow.

Expanding its range from the panhandle of Florida, this bird can be found breeding in north central Florida. Its preferred habitat is that of semi-open, wet, forested lands. In recent years it has become more adapted to humans, even sometimes nesting nearby human development.

The Mississippi Kite is fun to watch as it darts back and forth catching insects on the wing. It may also catch large insects on the ground and other small invertebrates, small reptiles, amphibians and mammals. Like the Cattle Egret and Cowbird, the Mississippi Kite follows herds of livestock in pastures to take advantage of the flushed insects.

Often using the same nest year after year, you will find them in tall trees. The nests are made of larger sticks and lined with finer material, including the abundant Spanish Moss. Two blue-white eggs are laid in early spring and hatch in about four-and-a-half weeks. The young are fed primarily insects and leave the nest in about five weeks. The winters are spent in South America.

The Snail Kite, formally called the "Everglade Kite," is found in freshwater marshes in the southern third of Florida. The Snail Kite is not typical of the other kites in that their wings are not slender and pointed. The male is slate-black with a white rump above and below the black tail. The female is dark-brown instead of black. Both sexes have red-orange faces and legs with a very black, hooked bill. This bill is used to extract the living part of Apple Snails from their shells. It is possible that Apple Snails are the only food the Snail Kite eats and is very susceptible to population fluctuations due to water levels.

The all-dark body with white rump makes this bird easy to spot in the right habitat of southern marshes and wetlands. In good breeding years these birds will raise two broods of four or five young each. In poor years nesting will fail completely, giving rise to the special concern status of this bird from year to year.

Mississippi Kite (bottom) and Snail Kite (top)

American Swallow-tailed Kite *Elanoides forficatus*

The largest of the kites, at two feet, the American Swallow-tailed Kite is also one of the easiest to recognize. This kite has a long, black, forked tail similar in shape to that of the Barn Swallow. The American Swallow-tailed Kite has a white head and neck. The back, wings and tail are black and the chest and belly are white. In flight the underwing is white in the forewing and black in the trailing edge of the wing. This bright contrast between the white and black, along with the long, split, swallow-like tail make it hard to mistake.

This bird also has a habit of perching on a bare branch to watch for prey. Even on perch he is quite striking. This kite takes water in the same manner as the Barn Swallow—by flying low over the surface and skimming drinks as it flies along.

Preferring wooded forests along wetlands and river bottoms, the American Swallow-tailed Kite can be found throughout Florida in the correct habitat from late winter until early fall. In the non-breeding season, they may be found as far north as the Great Lakes. Nesting also occurs along most of the Gulf states bordering Florida as well as South Carolina, Mississippi and Louisiana. The Swallow-tailed Kite spends the winter in South America.

The American Swallow-tailed Kite feeds on flying insects, making for spectacular and graceful flights. It will also glean some food from the branches of trees: lizards, snakes and insects. Seeming very comfortable in the air, many times the captured prey is eaten during flight.

Nesting occurs in tall trees with heavy foliage to conceal the nest. Often a nest will be added to from the previous year. The nest is quite substantial and is lined with soft plant materials and some feathers. Two white-brown mottled eggs are laid in the nest in late winter and are incubated for four weeks. The young are fed bits of food torn apart by the adults and whole insects as they grow larger. The nesting of the American Swallow-tailed Kite may be loosely colonial. The young are able to leave the nest in about six weeks. The young resemble the adults, except for a shorter tail and the primary wing feathers which may have white spots in them.

As in many of the birds dependant upon wetlands, the Swallow-tailed Kite has decreased in population and breeding range to mainly a few southern states. The population used to breed into the upper midwest, but because of extensive drainage of swamps and river bottoms for agricultural purposes the populations have been relegated to the deep south.

American Swallow-tailed Kite

Red-tailed Hawk *Buteo jamaicensis*

The Red-tailed Hawk is probably the most abundant, visible and recognizable of all the hawks. Although commonly called a "chicken hawk" by most rural people, it rarely captures chickens. The Red-tailed Hawk belongs to a group of raptors called *buteos*. These hawks are robust in shape, have shorter and broader wings and fairly wide tails which allow them to soar in thermals as they search for prey. The Red-tailed Hawk is not as well-adapted for pursuit as the accipitors and falcons although it is not as slow as vultures.

In Florida, the Red-tailed Hawk is usually seen soaring in the sky during the day or sitting on a perch in a tree or on a pole waiting for some unsuspecting prey. It prefers open country where it can soar and can be found in most habitats over the entire state as well as in all the south. The population in Florida increases during the winter months as the northern populations migrate south.

The Red-tailed Hawk stands about two feet tall and has a white breast with a line of spots across creating a "belly band." This band can be easily distinguished upon close observation, but from a distance it can be difficult to see. The adult birds have a rusty-red tail with a faint band at the end. This "red" tail is noticeable both at rest and while soaring.

Nesting occurs in the less inhabited areas of the state except for the extreme southern part of Florida and the Keys which may be due to the lack of trees in the Everglades and the high population of humans. Nests are placed in tall palms or trees in a platform nest of branches and twigs and are lined with finer plant material. Southern nests have a tendency to be closer to the ground than those in the north, possibly because of the lack of extremely tall trees in Florida.

Normally two eggs are laid in the nest in February and incubated for over five weeks. The young hatch a couple days apart and may remain in the nest for several weeks more. In poor hunting years, the youngest may lose out to an older chick, but this is less common than in other raptors. Immature birds do not exhibit the red tail but have gray tails with faint banding.

This "chicken hawk" is blamed for damage to livestock but in most cases it is not guilty. The normal diet for the Red-tailed Hawk is small rodents. It may also eat larger prey such as rabbits, rats, game birds, snakes and amphibians. The Red-tailed Hawk spots its prey, from a soaring position and then drops down to grasp the prey in its talons. It has adapted well to roadsides where mice and meadow voles are abundant. Most often the larger prey taken is ill or injured. Healthy, large prey can usually escape the Red-tailed Hawk.

Red-tailed Hawk

Red-shouldered Hawk   *Buteo lineatus*

The Red-shouldered Hawk is a common breeding hawk throughout Florida in the correct habitat. This hawk is smaller than the abundant Red-tailed Hawk. The Red-shouldered Hawk stands about eighteen-to-twenty inches tall and is not as robust in stature as the Red-tailed Hawk. The breast of the Red-shouldered Hawk is rusty-red in color. The shoulder has a darker-red patch which is not always easy to distinguish. However, the red shoulders are quite evident when seen from above or the bird is twisting and turning in flight. The tail is black with narrow, white bands which appear as alternate bands of narrow white and broad black. The head is dark and the legs are yellow. A variety of Red-shouldered Hawk that is smaller and lighter in color appears in southern Florida.

Wet forests and flood plain forests with mature canopies are the preferred habitat for this hawk. The forest will generally be near wetlands. The diet of the Red-shouldered Hawk is reptiles and amphibians. The Red-shouldered Hawk is one of the best snake-capturing hawks in the south. Sometimes it will bring more than a half dozen snakes to a nest a day. In Florida, lizards make up a good portion of its diet but become less importan further north. The Red-shouldered Hawk is also very proficient at capturing frogs, insects and crayfish. At certain times of the year rodents are a good portion of the diet.

Nests are usually built in the heavy crotch of tall trees. They can be substantial and are built from sticks, twigs and many other plant materials. The nest is lined with finer material such as grasses, Spanish moss and green vegetation. The nest is added to as incubation progresses. Nests are often used over and over again, or at least every couple of years if successful nesting has occurred.

Three and sometimes four eggs are laid in the nest in January and incubated for four weeks. The eggs are off-white with brown markings. The young are attended by both parents. The young are fed bits of prey at first but as they become older they are brought whole frogs and snakes to tear apart and devour. At certain times of the day an adult bird may shelter the young from the hot sun if the nest is open from above. The young are able to leave the nest in about six weeks. Nesting has become a prime consideration for these birds and they have become somewhat adapted to man if the proper nesting trees are available. Riparian woodlands have become more important as nesting sites in recent years.

Red-shouldered Hawk

Crested Caracara   *Caracara cheriway*

The Crested Caracara is a large bird of prey that belongs in its own group, the Caracara. The Caracaras are birds with long legs and faces that are featherless. This bird may appear almost eagle-like. One of the names for this bird is the "Mexican Eagle" and it is one of Mexico's symbols, much as the Bald Eagle is a symbol of the United States. This bird has a black crown that ends in a crest. The rest of the head is white except for the red, featherless face. The white of the head extends down the neck into the upper chest where it fades into the dark body. The legs are yellow.

In flight the Crested Caracara may appear to be an eagle because of the white head, but the Crested Caracara's tail has a heavy black band at the end. Also, in flight, the base of the primary feathers is light in color which gives white wing patches at the end of the wings similar to the Black Vulture.

This bird is found in open pasture land and wastelands in the central part of Florida. It prefers open, brushy areas with palmetto palms and cabbage palms where it feeds upon carrion as well as small prey such as lizards, large insects, small mammals and birds. It will not hesitate to steal carrion away from vultures. The Crested Caracara's long legs give it a similar appearance to the Bustard from Africa which also hunts on the ground for lizards.

The Crested Caracara can be seen on the ground, on fence posts, in palms, trees or on any perch that gives it a view of the surroundings. Outside this small portion of Florida, the only reliable place to see these birds is in Texas. This makes Florida a popular place to seek out the Crested Caracara. The population has diminished over the years, primarily due to agricultural practices which have taken up the scrub land upon which the Crested Caracara depends. However, in recent years the Crested Caracara has been seen in some cultivated areas indicating that they may be adapting to man.

Not a lot is known about the breeding cycle of the Crested Caracara, but they seem to prefer to place their nests high in either pines or palmetto. The nest is large and cup-shaped. It is usually built from sticks and palmetto branches along with assorted other branches that may be available.

Two to three pinkish-white eggs with brown markings are laid in the nest in early winter and they hatch in about four weeks. The young are able to leave the nest in about five or six weeks, although they may spend a great amount of time on the ground for a while. The young resemble the adults in color, except they are streaked with brown and do not have as defined a pattern of black and white.

Crested Caracara

American Kestrel *Falco sparverius*

The American Kestrel is the smallest of the falcons that breed in the United States and is the most distinctive in its markings and coloration. Also called the "Sparrow Hawk," this little falcon's population in Florida is made up of a separate race which is a bit smaller than the northern races of the American Kestrel. The Kestrel is found throughout Florida and is quite common, but less so in the extreme south. Some populations have decreased due to loss of nest cavities, but the use of Wood Duck boxes, holes in buildings and Kestrel boxes have helped this bird tremendously both in the north and Florida.

The Kestrel has adapted to man fairly well, making use of grassy roadsides and cultivated areas to locate its prey. The primary food of these small falcons is grasshoppers and other insects, especially during the summer. During the winter, small birds and mice will become a greater portion of their diet.

One way you can recognize a Kestrel is by the way it locates its prey. Usually the Kestrel will perch on a wire or post or some high advantage point and when a potential prey is spotted it will take off and "hover" above the spot. It then dives down, capture the prey in its talons and flies back to the perch to devour it. This is the only small bird of prey that does this in Florida.

The call of the Kestrel is a sharp *killy, killy, killy*, giving rise to another of its names, "Killy Hawk."

The best way to identify this falcon is by its striking coloration. Both sexes have rusty-colored backs and tails. The male's tail has only one large band at the tip. The female's tail has numerous narrow, black bands and a larger one at the tip. The female's wings are a russet-brown which matches her back, whereas the male's wings are a slate-blue-gray in color. Both sexes have very unique facial patterns. The top of the head is russet with a gray forehead. The face is white with two black, vertical stripes—one in front and one behind the eye.

The Kestrel nests in tree cavities. It has therefore been hurt by the loss of forests and trees due to agriculture and development. This falcon does take readily to nest boxes put out by man. After the success of Bluebird trails, many Audubon chapters have created Kestrel trails. Becoming accustomed to man, the Kestrel has learned to nest in cavities of abandoned buildings in suburban areas. Normally four young are reared in spring.

American Kestrel
Female (top)   Male (bottom)

Osprey *Pandion haliaetus*

Recovering from low populations in the middle of this century, the Osprey has become quite abundant in Florida where open water is prevalent. This "Fish Hawk," as it is many times called, is the most proficient of the fish-capturing birds of prey. It can be seen hovering above a body of water. The Osprey dives feet first into the water and most often comes up with a fairly large fish.

The talons of this bird of prey are highly maneuverable and when it transports a large fish the Osprey carries it parallel to its body so the length of the fish is in line with its body with the head most often pointing forward. This characteristic helps distinguish the Osprey from the Bald Eagle. The undersides of the Osprey differ from the Bald Eagle as well. The Osprey has a white front except for the tail. The Bald Eagle is dark on the front and the tail is white. The head of the Osprey is white except for a wide dark-brown eye-stripe, which also helps separate it from the Bald Eagle. The upper part of the body, wings and tail are dark-brown overall and the tail has faint bands running across it. A band of brown specks runs across the bottom of the neck. One of the most noticeable features of the Osprey in flight is the "black knuckles"—dark patches at the bend in the wing which makes the bend appear extremely pronounced.

The Osprey has taken readily to man-made towers and nest platforms, and nests in many areas where they have been placed. The most successful are those that are placed in areas of open water, especially those placed directly in the water. Nests that the birds build for themselves may be on telephone or utility poles, dead trees or some other high area. The nests are made of assorted materials. Since these nests are used for years they may become quite large, similar to the Bald Eagle's nests. These birds are not terribly territorial and the large nests may be quite close to each other.

Nesting occurs during late spring and often the same successful site will be used again and again. Usually three eggs are placed in the nest and incubation begins immediately, thereby causing the chicks to hatch a few days apart. Incubation lasts about five weeks. The young are fed regurgitated food from the male for the first week or so, then the female will tear apart fish for the chicks. The Osprey chicks will remain in the nest for about seven weeks before leaving to feed with the parents.

In Florida, the Osprey has become a bird of special concern and the number of nest platforms placed out on lakes and marshes has been increased. Wetland preservation is probably the most prudent way to ensure the survival of this fish-eating raptor.

Osprey

Wild Turkey *Meleagris gallopavo*

The Wild Turkey is the largest game bird in Florida as well as the rest of the United States. The Wild Turkey is smaller than the domestic turkey. It resembles the domestic Bronze Turkey because of the bronze-colored iridescent sheen of its dark feathers which makes this bird extremely beautiful when viewed up close. Standing almost four feet tall, the male is larger than the female and sports a red-and-blue featherless head which becomes brightly colored when in courtship display. The beak sports a knob of flesh called a "snerd" which becomes long and flashy during courtship antics. The size can become ten times longer than when in a non-excited stage. The male also has a tuft of feathers which is called a "beard." This tuft of feathers is more like a small horse tail hanging down from the center of the breast. Occasionally the female may have a beard. Females are about a foot shorter and do not have the brightly colored head.

The Wild Turkey can be found in forested wild areas. Its population is increasing in the correct habitat. In the forests it forages on seeds, nuts and insects. In some areas it has adapted well to agricultural fields that are adjacent to wild forested areas. In the northern part of the United States, as well as Florida, the agricultural areas are becoming a more important part of the Wild Turkey's habitat.

During the early spring the male turkeys strut about with their tails spread out like the proverbial Thanksgiving turkey and gobble to attract or locate females. This gobbling occurs normally during the early dawn hours. During March the female scrapes out a hidden nest and lines it sparsely with some leaves and vegetation. She will normally lay less than a dozen eggs but some northern broods may be one or two larger.

Incubation of the buff-colored eggs marked with light brown lasts about four weeks. The young are precocial and after drying for about a day they are able to leave the nest with the female. For the first part of the immature bird's life they forage in grassy openings or fields for insects. Females with broods of different ages may form loose groups of Wild Turkeys which can be quite impressive. To see a group of three or four hens with chicks of four different ages is quite a sight. Just seeing forty birds together is in itself remarkable.

Myakka River State Park is one of the areas where the Wild Turkey can be seen in Florida. In the early dawn hours they can be found roosting in trees. Care should be taken not to confuse them with vultures. During the day, the Wild Turkey can be found feeding in the forests or edges of fields. Many other state game areas and parks have the Wild Turkey.

Wild Turkey

Northern Bobwhite *Colinus virginianus*

Commonly called the "Quail" or "Bobwhite Quail," this bird gets its name from its loud call of *bob bob white*! About nine inches tall, the bobwhite is a reddish-brown ground-feeding bird. Its body is heavily mottled with crescents on each feather. Its head has a white eye-stripe with a white throat in the male and a buff-colored throat in the female. Both sexes may exhibit a crown when excited but the male's crest is more pronounced and darker than the female's. Preferring to run instead of fly, the Bobwhite can be seen scurrying about brushy areas. When surprised the Bobwhite will explode in a bombshell of rapid wing beats, usually unnerving the seeker.

In Florida, the Northern Bobwhite is found throughout the state in open forests, brushy areas, fields, and marginal agricultural areas, primarily cattle pastures. Except during breeding, the Northern Bobwhites will stay together as a group called a "covey." Most coveys are family groupings until fall when some will combine to make larger coveys.

In Florida, as in much of the south, the Bobwhite Quail is a game bird and is hunted extensively, usually with English Pointers. In restaurants, the Quail offered on the menus are those that have been farm-raised. Most states do not allow game to be sold, and it would not be very economical in most cases to use hunted birds.

The female builds a nest in grassy vegetation with a hood over it that has a side entrance. The nest is made from grasses and fine vegetation. Nesting begins in February with fourteen to fifteen eggs being laid. Incubation takes about three-and-a-half weeks with the chicks able to follow the female after drying out. The chicks are attended by both parents and are about the size of large bumblebees. Young quail chicks are very vulnerable at this age and are brooded by the female frequently during the cooler parts of the day.

Young quail will go through a series of molts before taking on the adult plumage. The young will be capable of short quick flights in about four weeks. It is at this time that some merging of larger coveys occurs. When at rest, especially at night, the members of the covey sleep with their heads pointing outward, probably for protection. If startled they will literally explode in all directions of the circle. A telltale sign of roosting coveys is an extensive group of black-and-white droppings.

The adult and young birds eat a variety of different types of food. Young insects are a major part of the diet but seeds, berries and other invertebrates are all eaten extensively.

Northern Bobwhite

Limpkin *Aramus guarauna*

Although not a terribly common bird, the Limpkin is truly a bird of Florida. When seen it is impressive and is not easily forgotten. It is found in wooded, freshwater areas found predominately in the interior parts of Florida where freshwater streams, lakes and swamps are located. It is less common in marshes. A small breeding population can be found in Georgia. This large bird was hunted extensively and populations were depleted until hunting them was banned. Since the last century their populations have increased.

Standing at just over two feet tall, this large wading bird is a brown color overall with white streaks over the body. The streaks are oblong spots that are pointed at the lower edge, making them almost teardrop-shaped but hanging upside down. The streaks are most abundant at the neck and are absent on the lower wings and tail. The head is light-colored and has a faint eye-ring. The bill is long, down-curved and yellow with a black tip. The Limpkin appears similar to an ibis from a distance although it has a bit shorter bill. No ibis has streaks, so upon a closer view they can be easily identified. If the feet are visible (but most often they are not), they are a dull-green color.

The breeding habits of the Limpkin are not as well-known as many of the other wetland species.

Evidently the Limpkin nests throughout the year, taking advantage of available abundant food sources. Because of this, two, possibly three broods are thought to be produced, although this is not well documented. The nests can be quite varied, being placed upon the ground as well as in shrubs and trees to a substantial height. The nests are almost always near water and woven with marsh vegetation such as rushes, reeds and grasses. It can be well hidden under brushy overhangs or in dense clusters of marsh vegetation.

Normally eight pale eggs are laid, taking about three weeks to hatch. The young after a short time are able to follow the mother and forage. Immature birds are similar in color to the adults, except they are lighter in color overall.

The Limpkin is especially adapted to eat its main food source: snails. Its bill does not match up top to bottom and the end is a bit curved so that it can pry snails from their shells. The Limpkin also eat many crustaceans, reptiles, amphibians, mollusks and aquatic insects. Snails are however the most important food source for this bird and it is therefore very susceptible to population fluctuations due to drought.

Limpkin

Sandhill Crane   *Grus canadensis*

Two subspecies of the Sandhill Crane can be found in Florida. The smaller, the Florida Sandhill Crane, is a resident bird whereas the Greater Sandhill Crane migrates from the north during the winter months. This bird is a resident of wet, grassy areas and marshes throughout Florida. Two areas where the Sandhill Crane can be found are Paynes Prairie State Preserve and Kissimmee Prairie. In winter the population of Sandhill Cranes quadruples with the influx of northern birds. Even though it prefers wet areas, the Sandhill Crane has adapted well to man's ways. At any time of the year you can see these birds in old fields, pastures, weed fields and even water hazards on golf courses. They have learned to glean grain from farmlands and can be seen in increasing numbers on agricultural lands.

The Sandhill Crane stands three-and-a-half to four feet tall. This large bird is gray in color with long legs and a long neck. The immature birds have a rust-brown wash over the head and upper body. Adult birds have a white cheek and a red forehead and crown. While wading or walking, the rump of the Sandhill Crane appears as though it has a "bustle" or hump hanging down. Frequently this bird is confused with the Great Blue Heron because of its color and size. Many people even mistakenly call the Great Blue Heron a "crane." Two easy ways to identify the Sandhill Crane is the tail and bustle. In flight, the Sandhill Crane flies with its neck outstretched while the Great Blue Heron pulls it head back into an "S" shape.

As with many of the wetland birds, the Sandhill Crane was hunted extensively and populations plummeted. The ban on hunting these birds has caused their populations to rebound quite well. Today the primary concern is the loss of wetlands.

The Sandhill Crane is omnivorous, feeding upon anything edible. It feeds in marshes taking anything that moves as well as seeds, berries and tubers. In dry areas it will feed on grain, insects, small mammals, birds and reptiles.

The nests of the Sandhill Crane are built in marshes upon piles of marsh vegetation hidden in dense foliage. In Florida, nesting occurs during the winter where rains aid in nest protection. Two mottled, buff-colored eggs are lain and hatch in about four weeks. The young birds follow the adults after a few days and forage with them until the fall. Sibling rivalry may eliminate one of the chicks in the brood.

The Sandhill Crane is related to the extinct Whooping Crane of Florida. Luckily a flock of Whooping Cranes is viable in Texas. Grand hopes of introducing the Whooping Crane into Florida are about to become a reality.

Sandhill Crane

King Rail   *Rallus elegans*

This large rail is a permanent resident in Florida and is found in thick marshes where it breeds. Rails are smaller marsh birds and are very secretive. They blend in with the vegetation very well and prefer to run rather than fly. The rails have short tails and streaking and stripes that make them blend in with marsh vegetation, especially vegetation that is old and dead. The wings of rails are short and rounded so that flight seems awkward and difficult for these birds. It has been said that, "Rails don't fly south, they walk" because their flight is not a graceful sight.

The King Rail is the largest rail in Florida, standing about fifteen inches tall. The King Rail is a rust-brown color overall and darker brown above. The upper breast is a clear-rust color and its black flanks are heavily-streaked with vertical stripes, giving it a barred look. Its back has buff-colored markings. The bill is long, slightly down-turned at the end, and nearly as long as twice the width of the head. One way to see if this bird is present is to give a sharp loud cough or just clap your hands. Often the King Rail will return with its call, a *kak kak kak* or *chuck chuck chuck*. Often it will just grunt back. This calling occurs mostly during the night or at dawn and during the hours of dusk, though sometimes you can get an answer during the middle of the day.

The King Rail prefers freshwater and its nest is built in heavy vegetation on small rises of land or mounds of vegetation. The nest is made of dried plant material of what is predominately in the area. The nest is quite elaborate and is bowl-shaped. About a dozen buff-colored, spotted eggs are laid in the nest beginning in January. The incubation lasts about three weeks and as soon as the chicks are dry, usually a day, they can forage with the mother. The chicks may remain with the mother for as long as two months.

The chicks are taught to forage in marshes for various aquatic insects as well as a variety of crustaceans. Seeds and berries can be a portion of the diet and adults will eat frogs and salamanders. In the winter, especially in north Florida, the diet is mainly seeds or grains.

The King Rail is often confused with the Clapper Rail but it is a bit larger than the Clapper Rail and the Clapper Rail is not nearly as brown and has a gray head and cheeks. The streaking on the back is more pronounced than on the back of the Clapper Rail. These rails, as well as all the rails in Florida, are on the concerned list because of the loss of wetlands.

King Rail

Clapper Rail   *Rallus longirostris*

Similar to the King Rail except that it is a bit smaller, the Clapper Rail is a rail of the coasts preferring brackish and saltwater marshes. The J. N. "Ding" Darling National Wildlife Refuge on Sanibel Island is a favorite place to find this elusive rail. In fact, you can't go wrong looking for many of the favorite birds of Florida in the Darling National Wildlife Refuge. One of the ways to distinguish the Clapper Rail from the King Rail is that the Clapper Rail's feathers have grey edges instead of the buff-colored edges of the larger King Rail, and the Clapper is more grey overall. The underside of the tail of the Clapper Rail is much more white than that of the King Rail and even appears to be all-white from a distance. However, the King Rail is less than an inch larger than the Clapper Rail so size is not really a distinguishing factor in general.

The Clapper Rail is a coastal bird found from Texas to Cape Cod. Where the King Rail and Clapper Rail are found together there may be some hybridization. Populations of the Clapper Rail, as in all the rails, have come under increased pressure due to the destruction of wetlands, land development and use of pesticides.

The Clapper Rail's nest is similar to that of the King Rail, being placed upon a high spot in a marsh, usually on dry ground. It is constructed of whatever marsh vegetation is available and some grasses. A hood is frequently made to protect the nest from overhead predation. The nest is deeply-cupped like a basket and is lined with fine, dry grasses. Usually ten brown-marked, buff-colored eggs are laid in the nest in early spring and will be incubated for about three weeks. Incubation begins soon after the first eggs are hatched so the chicks will hatch a few days apart. Brooding will continue for a week or longer to allow the chicks to be able to follow the adults and feed. The chicks will remain with the adults for nearly two months. By early summer they will be on their own.

The Clapper Rail prefers crustaceans, aquatic insects and other invertebrates, but it is omnivorous and will eat just about anything. The Clapper Rail is particularly fond of small crabs and their long bill makes them adept at capturing them. They are also able to probe for worms and mollusks in the soft soils of the marsh. Berries and seeds augment their diet especially during the winter months.

As with the King Rail, the Clapper Rail is most often identified by its call, cackling *kek kek kek kek* or *cak cak cak cak* repeatedly, picking up speed and then slowing down at the end. The calls are most often at the hours of dawn and dusk.

Clapper Rail

Common Moorhen *Gallinula chloropus*

The Common Moorhen, or Common Gallinule as was previously called, is quite abundant in the wetlands throughout Florida, especially the interior. It can be found in freshwater marshes, ponds, lake edges, and less commonly, in brackish and saltwater areas. It prefers the edges of the water where it can make use of vegetation in which to hide and feed. The Common Moorhen can, however, be found at times swimming out in the open water.

This bird is relatively large at just over a foot tall and is not terribly shy as are so many of the marsh birds we have discussed so far. This chicken-like bird can easily be seen in most natural areas and can be studied if it is not approached too closely. It is not afraid of humans.

Although not as brightly colored as the Purple Gallinule, the Common Moorhen is quite a handsome bird. About fourteen inches tall, the Common Moorhen stands erect like the barnyard chicken and has large feet, similar to the chicken. Actually, the toes of the Common Moorhen are quite a bit longer which aids it in walking over the marsh vegetation where it feeds. The bird is slate-black over the front with a darker head and neck. The back is an olive-brown. The most striking and easiest characteristic that can be used to identify this bird is the red facial shield that goes from the bill up onto the forehead. The bill is also red with a yellow tip. The flanks have a white stripe and the under-tail feathers are white which it flicks about as it walks about searching for food. While swimming the Common Gallinule pushes its head forward as if pumping the body along with the head push. The legs and toes are yellow with a reddish band on the legs above the uppermost joint. The rare Purple Gallinule is similar, except quite purple in color and the forehead shield is blue above the red bill.

The Common Moorhen eats a variety of marsh plants as well as seeds, insects, crustaceans and small mollusks. During the season berries can be a substantial part of the Common Moorhen's diet.

Nests are usually constructed in the water on a mound or a floating mat. They are constructed of marsh vegetation, usually cattails and reeds. Occasionally the nest will be constructed in shrubs or on land, but this allows more predation of the nest to occur.

The buff-colored eggs are marked with brown and are laid during late winter to early spring. Eight to twelve eggs are laid in the nest and incubation lasts about three weeks. In Florida and parts of the south, two broods are not uncommon with the juveniles from the first brood assisting with the second brood. The chicks are all black and able to leave the nest when dried and forage with the parents.

Common Moorhen

American Coot   *Fulica americana*

Most abundant during the winter, the American Coot is found nesting in Florida, primarily in the interior on freshwater marshes, lakes, ponds and backwaters of rivers. The Mud Hen as it is sometimes called is not common in the Keys. The Florida population is heavily augmented during the winter from northern populations, making this bird one of the most abundant in open water areas.

The American Coot is similar in shape to that of the Purple and Common Gallinules, except that it is more duck-shaped and tends to frequent open water. The American Coot is a dark-gray overall with an almost black head. The American Coot has a white bill and white rump patch that appears on each side of the rump. The upper part of the bill or shield is a deep-red or orange, almost appearing as a knob. Occasionally an American Coot may exhibit a whitish shield, which may indicate that it is a Caribbean Coot or hybrid. However, further studies have shown that many Coots exhibit the white shield. In flight, the American Coot exhibits narrow, white, trailing edges on its wings. The toes of the American Coot are lobed, almost appearing webbed, but they are still divided like the foot of the chicken. Perhaps this is one reason it is called "mud hen." The legs in the adults are a yellowish-green and those of the immature birds are dark.

Usually feeding in groups, the American Coot's diet is heavily concentrated on aquatic vegetation; it is therefore usually found in shallow water. Although it feeds primarily on plants, the Coot will also eat aquatic insects, crustaceans and snails. The American Coot is a good swimmer and can also catch fish, tadpoles and other fast swimmers. The American Coot is not above stealing food from other water birds. In the north some Coots will remain as long as the water remains unfrozen, but the bulk of them migrate to the south where they can reach huge populations, even becoming a problem by leaving huge amounts of tell-tale signs along banks of park and golf course lakes.

Nests are placed in areas of emerging vegetation and a floating platform of vegetation is anchored around the nest. Dummy nests may be made, with only one used for egg-laying. The others may be used for courting or resting with newly-hatched young.

About ten buff-colored eggs marked with brown are laid and incubation takes three-and-a-half weeks. Nesting may begin in March and those nests that are successful may allow a second brood. Research indicates that the American Coot can recognize its eggs from those of a duck that wishes to parasitize the nest with its own eggs. Nests that have duck eggs left in them are not successful.

American Coot

Purple Gallinule *Porphyrula martinica*

This striking bird is like something out of the tropics with its bright iridescent-purple color. The Purple Gallinule is truly a southern bird found only in Florida and the Gulf Coast to Texas and up the Atlantic Coast to South Carolina. Stragglers may occur further north. In Florida it is a bird of freshwater lake edges, swamps, marshes and river backwaters. It is not as abundant as the Common Moorhen but can be found all over the state in the correct habitat. During the winter, the northern part of Florida is usually devoid of these birds as they move south. Good places to locate these birds are the Everglades, Shark Valley and Myakka River State Park, although any good wetland that is protected can harbor these incredible birds.

The purple color is so rich that it almost seems painted on the bird. The purple is located on the head, neck, and front of the bird while its back is a green-olive color, somewhat iridescent in appearance. The bill, similar to the Common Moorhen, is red with a yellow tip but the forehead shield is sky-blue. The legs are yellow but are missing the red above the top joint as in the Common Moorhen. The undertail coverts are all white, making it easy to identify as it swims away. The toes of the Purple Gallinule are long, which allows this bird to walk across aquatic vegetation and turn over lily leaves to locate snails and aquatic insects.

The primary diet of the Purple Gallinule is seeds, berries and aquatic vegetation but it is opportunistic and sometimes takes larger prey such as amphibians and small birds. They seem to be more varied in their diet than the Common Moorhen. After the breeding season, seeds and berries seem to become a more important part of the diet, possibly because of increased availability.

Being somewhat more secretive, the nests of the Purple Gallinule are usually found over deeper water than that of the Common Moorhen. The floating mat is quite extensively woven together with standing vegetation. It is hollowed out, with a partial hood covering the nest.

About eight eggs are laid in the nest and are incubated for about three to three-and-a-half weeks. The eggs are a rich-buff color, marked with brown. Like the Common Moorhen, the young from the first brood will help with the nesting of the second brood by defending territory and chicks. In both types of Gallinules, the nests may have a platform or ramp that is used by the birds to walk into the water. The call of the Purple Gallinule is a *cluck, cluck, cluck, cluck* similar to that of the Common Moorhen or barnyard chicken. The call can be quite rapid at first slowing down at the end to a *cluck* or two.

Purple Gallinule

American Avocet   *Recurvirostra americana*

Although the American Avocet does not breed in Florida, it can be seen in increasing numbers during spring and autumn migration. It also occasionally spends the winter months in Florida. The American Avocet is a bird that breeds primarily in the western United States and a few isolated east coast areas of the Carolinas. It can be found in shallow water areas of fields, marshes and lakes. It can sometimes be found feeding in agricultural fields.

In breeding plumage this bird is quite beautiful. Unfortunately, the winter plumage is not nearly as striking and this is what Florida birders see. This foot-and-a-half tall bird has long legs used to wade about the marshes in which it feeds. The bill is extremely long and thin. It is upturned and appears somewhat bent at the outer end. The body of the American Avocet is slender and is striking in its black-and-white markings. The body is white and the wings at rest have two wide, horizontal black bars. In flight the wings have black primaries and the secondaries have white leading and trailing edges. Also in flight there are two black stripes down the back. The legs are gray in color. The adult plumage is a deep yellow-rust color on the chest, neck and head. On winter and juvenile birds, grey replaces the rust and is the prominent color of the birds found in Florida.

Avocets feed by sweeping their long, thin bill back and forth while walking forward, feeling for their food. In deeper water, the Avocet can be seen feeding with its head completely beneath the surface. The Avocet in flight or when excited gives off a loud clear *keet keet keet.* Upon landing, it walks about bobbing its head and calling repeatedly for a short time.

Avocets feed mainly on aquatic insects, crustaceans, mollusks and other invertebrates. The Avocet will eat seeds, small plants and algae as well.

The American Avocet can be found with other wading migrants from the north in small groups. Good places to see this bird are Merritt Island National Wildlife Refuge, Myakka River State Park and J. N. "Ding" Darling National Wildlife Refuge. This bird prefers coastal areas but in recent years reports of their appearance in the interior are becoming more numerous. Most of the bays along the coast are potential areas to see the American Avocet. Popular bays are located at Tampa Bay, Bradenton and the Keys.

American Avocet

American Oystercatcher   *Haematopus palliatus*

Entirely a bird of the coasts, the American Oystercatcher is more abundant on the Gulf coast than the Atlantic coast. Although its populations have decreased greatly since the turn-of-the-century, the American Oystercatcher seems to be holding its own, especially on the Gulf Coast. It breeds northward almost to Cape Cod. The population along the Gulf Coast is spotty with most breeding populations located in Texas.

This rather large-bodied shorebird is about a foot-and-a-half tall and is quite striking if you see it feeding along the coasts of Florida. The most noticeable feature of these noisy shorebirds is the large, red-orange bill. The bill is flattened to allow it to pry apart the shells of mollusks. The Oystercatcher has a black head with yellow eyes surrounded by a red eye-ring. The back of the Oystercatcher is dark-brown and the front is white. The wings show a white bar at rest and quite prominent white patches on the wings and upper rump while in flight. The legs are rather short for a shorebird and are flesh-colored with short, fat toes. Young birds are brown over the head, the bill is not nearly as red and the back is mottled.

The American Oystercatcher feeds extensively upon oysters, clams and mussels. Its flattened bill also makes it adept at taking the insides out of sea cucumbers, starfish and sea urchins. They are fond of larger crustaceans such as crabs, crayfish and shrimp. While they are feeding along the shoreline they will take worms and fish caught in tidal pools left as the tide goes out. Often when feeding, the Oystercatcher will take the prey out of the water and go ashore to finish eating it so that it won't be lost or swim away. Oystercatchers have learned to force mollusks and other potential food into the crevices of rocks to hold them while eating the soft insides.

Nests are made in shallowed-out depressions in sand or gravel along coastal shorelines. Usually the nest is out in the open where little vegetation exists. Nest predation by gulls, raccoons and feral animals can be quite severe. Nesting may be attempted several times.

Two to three lightly-marked olive-colored eggs are laid in the scrape and incubated for about four weeks by both parents. The chicks are able to follow the parents after a short time but will remain dependent upon them for a long time as they learn to use their strangely-shaped bills to open mollusks.

94

American Oystercatcher

Black-necked Stilt *Himantopus mexicanus*

This tall, slim wading bird is found throughout Florida in fresh and saltwater wetlands. The Black-necked Stilt has become more numerous during the last half of this century. The Black-necked Stilt breeds locally in the West in a variety of habitats. The northern part of Florida usually is devoid of these birds during the winter as many migrate to South America. The Stilt is most common in the lower two-thirds of Florida and the lower third during the winter.

The bright-red, long, thin legs make this bird almost unmistakable. At fifteen inches tall, the Black-necked Stilt seems to be all legs. The Stilt is black above and white below with a white face. A white spot above the eye is prominent. Couple this with a sharp, black, needle-like bill and you have a Black-necked Stilt. In flight the wings are black, accenting the white rump and underparts and the long, red legs hang straight out behind the Stilt, making it easy to identify. The juveniles and female birds have browner backs than the bright black of the males.

The Black-necked Stilt is very vocal giving a *kep kep kep kep* call when feeding and even in flight. The Stilt will usually be found in small groups numbering less than a dozen, except during heavy migration.

Utilizing both fresh and saltwater habitats, the Black-necked Stilt can be seen feeding in shallow water. It can be found probing the shallow water of marshes, wet fields and lake edges. The primary food of the Stilt is all types of aquatic insects, crustaceans, worms and small mollusks. It will also take fish, tadpoles, small crabs and crayfish. Seeds and aquatic vegetation are eaten but they are not a significant part of its diet.

Nesting begins in April and may last until the end of summer. Four speckled eggs are laid in a nest placed above the water. The Stilt on the nest is a sight to see as it folds its long, red legs to nestle itself on the eggs. Nesting is sometimes in loose colonies where a dozen or more may be in close proximity.

The eggs are incubated for about three-and-a-half weeks. Adult birds will deliberately wet their feathers to keep humidity of the eggs high, especially during hot weather. If the eggs dry out, the chicks will not be able to break out of the shell and will perish. Both parents take turns at incubation and caring for the chicks. The chicks are able to follow the adults after drying and will remain with them for about another month.

Black-necked Stilt

Semipalmated Plover *Charadrius semipalmatus*

Plovers are wading birds that vary in size from six or seven inches tall to over a foot tall. They are more compact than sandpipers with short, thick necks and short, thick bills. The populations of the Semipalmated Plover in Florida are at a maximum during the migration periods of fall and spring, but it can also be found in good numbers during the winter as well. Since many Plovers migrate early in the season, the Semipalmated Plover may return to Florida as early as July. The month with the least number of Plovers is June when the breeding birds are nesting in the extreme tundra portions of North America.

The Semipalmated Plover is a small plover at just over seven inches tall. During the winter, the plover's plumage is less spectacular than during breeding and the Semipalmated Plover is no different. The Semipalmated Plover has a brown back with a white belly and front. The legs are yellow-orange in color, with the winter legs more yellow than orange. Young birds have almost gray legs. The short bill is somewhat yellow at the base and the tip is dark. Two characteristics that help identify the Semipalmated Plover are the single band across the lower neck and the facial pattern. The head is brown with a white forehead patch which extends to make a white eye-line. The throat is white. A wide, brown band goes across the face from the bill and merges with the brown on the head. The name "Semipalmated" comes from the partial webbing between the toes.

The plovers prefer the wet shorelines of both freshwater mud flats and saltwater tidal flats. These birds can be found at the waters edge, in the wet, sandy areas or even further up away from the wet soils. The plover feeds differently than many of the sandpipers, running in short spurts with their head held erect, a characteristic of many plovers.

The Semipalmated Plover feeds on small insects, worms and crustaceans it finds in the sandy shoreline and mud flats. Small mollusks make up a good portion of its diet in wet flats, as well as insects and crustaceans found in the wash line.

The populations of the Semipalmated Plover are recovering from the hunting pressure at the turn-of-the-century, but it is still under increasing pressure due to lack of feeding areas during migration.

Semipalmated Plover
Summer plumage (bottom)

Black-bellied Plover *Pluvialis squatarola*

The Black-bellied Plover is the largest plover to winter in Florida and can be quite abundant, especially on the coasts. Similar to the Semipalmated Plover, the Black-bellied Plover nests in the tundra of Canada and Alaska and spends the winter in the lower coastal states and Florida. It will also winter as far south as South America. In Florida it is most common from late July until migration is complete in May. Although the bulk of the birds leave Florida by May these birds can still be found in all seasons, although June and July have the least amount . One reason that some birds remain in Florida during the summer is that it takes a couple of years for the Black-bellied Plover to reach breeding age.

In Florida, this bird can be found feeding along coastal beaches as well as inland on the beaches of lakes and rivers. Occasionally the Black-belled Plover can be found foraging in agricultural fields, especially during migration.

Typical of the plovers, the Black-bellied Plover has a stocky body with a small neck and small, black bill. The plumage in winter is dramatically different than that of the breeding season. In breeding plumage, the belly, face and chest are dark-black and the rump is white. In winter plumage, the colors are an extremely muted gray. The most identifiable characteristic is seen in flight. The wings have faint, white wing patterns. The "pits" at the underside base of the wings are black in color, which differentiates the Black-bellied Plover from other plovers or the sandpipers.

The Black-bellied Plover feeds on small mollusks and crustaceans. It will also eat whatever insects and microorganisms it can find at the wash line. Worms and insects are probed for in soft soils both inland and in mud flats. During migration it is very opportunistic, even eating some grain products. Feeding may be quite competitive and territories will be defended.

One way to tell the Black-bellied Plover from the sandpipers and the Golden Plover is its call. The Black-bellied Plover gives a three-noted, clear whistle with the middle note being slightly lower pitched. This call is given in flight or when it takes off after being frightened. The call can be heard a good distance. Calling occurs more often in flight than while on the ground.

Black-bellied Plover
Summer plumage (bottom)

Killdeer   *Charadrius vociferus*

Probably the best-known and most common of the plovers, the Killdeer is found over all of Florida as well as the rest of the eastern United States. Of the "ringed" plovers (that is, having one or more black rings around the neck), it is the largest. The Killdeer breeds throughout Florida in old fields, agricultural lands, meadows and pastures. Considered a shorebird, the Killdeer does not need a shoreline to thrive and is doing quite well in areas developed by humans. Populations greatly increase during the winter months as migrants from the north flow into Florida.

Two rings, or black bands, across its chest distinguishes the Killdeer from the Semipalmated Plover and Wilson's Plover, which have only one band. Also, the Killdeer is the larger of the three being ten to eleven inches tall, although it is a bit slimmer. The Killdeer has a beautiful golden-brown rump that is quite pronounced when in flight. The wings have white markings similar to the Semipalmated and Wilson's Plovers. The Killdeer's tail is proportionately longer than the other two small plovers. Probably the easiest way to distinguish the Killdeer from the other plovers is by its call: *killdeer killdeer killdeer*, which it gives loudly in flight as well as on the ground. It will also give a loud *dee* call when disturbed or even a *dee dee dee*.

Nesting occurs in almost any undisturbed open area in agricultural lands as well as suburban areas. A scrape is made where there is a mixture of stones and little vegetation and usually four eggs are laid in the nest. Nesting begins in March and incubation takes about four weeks. The eggs are extremely well-camouflaged, being buff-colored with heavy brown markings. The young are able to follow the parents soon after hatching and remain with both parents for another month.

During incubation and rearing of young the adults are extremely protective. The adult Killdeer sometimes feigns injury by calling loudly, stretching out its wing and fanning its tail and flopping about on the ground in order to lure a potential predator away. As the predator is lured further and further away from the nest or chicks the bird seems to become less and less injured, finally flying away when safety is achieved.

The Killdeer eats a variety of insects but will also take a number of seeds. During the rearing of young, insects are the primary food. In the far north the Killdeer can remain longer into the cold season because it will eat seeds, unlike many shorebirds.

Killdeer

Wilson's Plover *Charadrius wilsonia*

Similar in size to the Semipalmated Plover, the Wilson's Plover is a nesting species in Florida. This small plover is found almost commonly and exclusively on the shores and beaches of the coasts of Florida. North Florida is not as populated but receives an influx during winter from northern migrants. It appears that northern migrants prefer the Gulf coast as opposed to the Atlantic coast. During winter, the entire coastline from Texas to the Carolinas, attracts these small plovers.

Another of the "ringed" plovers, the Wilson's Plover has a larger, single black band than does the Semipalmated Plover. It also has a larger bill which is black. The legs are a flesh-colored gray. The winter plumage is similar to the Semipalmated Plover except for the bill, legs and neck band.

Nesting occurs in April and May on beaches of sand, small stones or even gravel roofs. Usually the nest is placed where a variety of objects are scattered about to help disguise it. The nest may be filled with bits of vegetation, sticks or stones. Like the Killdeer, Wilson's Plover lays three or four buff-colored, heavily-marked eggs. Incubation takes three-and-a-half weeks with both parents in attendance. The chicks are able to follow the parents soon after hatching and drying. As in the Killdeer, the parents are very adept at feigning injury to lure predators away from the eggs and chicks. It will take three or four weeks for the young plovers to become self-sufficient.

Primarily a coastline feeder, the Wilson's Plover eats crustaceans, especially small crabs. This plover also feeds on numerous insects and on small worms found in the wet sand of beaches. Wilson's Plover can also be found feeding on sandbars and in tidal pools where it captures stranded insects and crustaceans. After major storms, you can see them taking advantage of the water line organisms that have been washed up on the beach. You may find this small bird feeding most of the day and night along the water's edge.

The Wilson's Plover is a solitary feeder during the winter unlike many sandpipers and other shorebirds. The Wilson's Plover will defend a feeding territory from other Wilson's Plovers which explains why you do not see groups of these birds while strolling the beaches. In in all the plovers, large groups are the exception rather than the rule.

Wilson's Plover
Female (top)   Male (bottom)

Greater Yellowlegs *Tringa melanoleuca*

Nesting in the tundra, the Greater Yellowlegs is a common winter resident in Florida. Some of these long-legged waders appear to remain for the entire year. This wading bird can be found along shorelines of freshwater lakes and marshes as well as saltwater areas. It can also be found in flooded fields and river backwaters. The Greater Yellowlegs is usually found singly or in small groups during the winter because it defends a winter feeding territory similar to the Wilson's Plover. These birds can be found all through the southern coastlines from Virginia to Texas during the winter months.

The Greater Yellowlegs is a rather tall shorebird at about fourteen inches tall. As its name implies the long legs are yellow, its most striking feature. The bill is long, black, thin and slightly upturned at the end. The bill can be lighter in color near the head. The Yellowlegs is gray overall, being lighter on the undersides. In flight, the back is dark and the rump is white with slight bars across the tail although the tail still appears white. The gray back and flanks are checkered. The cheek is darker gray and a white eye-line is faintly visible. In winter plumage they appear lighter overall but as migration begins heavier colors and markings begin to appear.

Lesser Yellowlegs are smaller by about four inches, their bill is shorter and slimmer and the knee joints are not as thick. Another way to tell the Lesser and Greater Yellowlegs apart is to listen to the call. Even though it is similar, the Greater Yellowleg's calls are grouped in three to five calls, whereas the Lesser Yellowlegs only gives the call one to three times. Also, if the body size is similar to that of the Robin it is a Lessor Yellowlegs.

The Greater Yellowlegs feeds by wading through the shallow water of lakes and marshes probing for its food. The food it seeks is quite varied. It will take small minnows, crustaceans, insects, mollusks and a host of other aquatic organisms. During migration it will take berries and seeds but the preferred food is aquatic organisms. Occasionally it will skim the surface of the water for insects that are emerging or that have been blown into the water. Unlike the plovers, the Yellowlegs do not like to feed out of the water and may even wade in the water up to their body. The body size keeps the two Yellowlegs from directly competing with each other because they feed at different water depths.

Greater Yellowlegs

Whimbrel *Numenius phaeopus*

The Whimbrel and Long-billed Curlew are very similar in size and appearance. They are also very large and easy to see. The Whimbrel is a common bird found in Florida during the winter and during migration. The Whimbrel normally winters in South America and is less abundant during the months November through February. It is almost absent during the summer. Its preferred habitat is mud flats, marshes, beaches and wet fields. Not found extensively in the interior, the Whimbrel prefers the coastlines. During the winter the Whimbrel can be found from Florida up the Atlantic coast into the Carolinas and in Louisiana and Texas. In migration it will frequent almost any kind of wet area where it can feed and even has been found in wet pastures and agricultural fields.

The Whimbrel is brown overall with mottling and reaches a height of a foot-and-a-half. The underside is lighter brown with faint mottling. Most pronounced is the Whimbrel's long, down-curved bill used to probe for food. However, the Whimbrel's bill is not as long as the Curlew's bill. The head is striped with dark brown with a dark eye-stripe. This striping is absent in the Long-billed Curlew. In flight, the Whimbrel's rump is dark as well as the underside of the wings. The legs are blue-gray similar to that of the Long-billed Curlew.

The food of the Whimbrel is aquatic insects, crustaceans, mollusks and other aquatic organisms. They also eat fish, worms and tadpoles. In migration, the diet can become quite varied as the Whimbrel find themselves in dry fields, lawns and pastures. Insects, berries and seeds then become more important as a food source. The Whimbrel feeds in small groups of up to a half-dozen individuals. They may also feed in groups with other waders like vurlews, dandpipers, willets, yellowlegs and plovers.

The call of the Whimbrel is a series of short rapid whistles numbering from five to seven. The whistles are of one pitch: *te te te te te te*. The calls are most often given in flight when the birds are flying in a single line.

Taking up to three years to become of breeding age, the juvenile Whimbrel may be found in unusual places such as shopping centers, golf courses and city parks. When this occurs, especially in the more urban areas, they create quite a stir.

Whimbrel

Long-billed Curlew *Numenius americanus*

The Long-billed Curlew is not terribly common but is fairly regular in its visits to Florida. It is often confused with the Whimbrel. The Long-billed Curlew is a winter visitor but can be found in the state from September until May. It is found mostly along the coasts of Florida and up into the Carolinas. It then is absent for the most part until you get to Louisiana and Texas. Breeding occurs in the western prairie states. In Florida, you may find this bird on the coastal beaches and mud flats probing for invertebrates with its long down-curved bill. It is less common on the Gulf coast than the Atlantic coast.

The Long-billed Curlew is nearly six inches taller than the Whimbrel and has a much longer bill, about nine inches long. The primary difference other than size between the Long-billed Curlew and the Whimbrel is the lack of marked stripes on the head of the Long-billed Curlew. The Long-billed Curlew is more of a brown color than the Whimbrel and flashes reddish-brown inner wing linings when it flies. A bird that may exhibit the same wing linings is the Marbled Godwit, but its bill is shorter and is up-turned instead of down-turned.

The Curlew's call is one reason it may have received its name. The call is a loud, sweet, ascending *cur lee* or a long, drawn-out *kurleeeeeuuuu.*

When it is disturbed it gives a quick *ki li li li.*

Because of its long, down-curved bill the Curlew is extremely adept at getting worms and crustaceans from their long burrows in the mud and soil. The Long-billed Curlew will also eat insects found in the mud flats and wet soils of the beaches that it frequents. Being a rather large bird it can take some of the larger crustaceans and mollusks that are left by other shorebirds. Tadpoles, small frogs, fish and even young birds make up this opportunistic bird's diet. In some agricultural fields it frequents in migration the Long-billed Curlew may feed on seeds and berries.

Since the breeding age of these birds seems to begin at three years of age, occasionally the Long-billed Curlew can be seen during the summer months and non-breeding adults may show up in various parts of the United States at odd seasons. The populations of the Curlews have been hurt because of loss of breeding habitat which has shrunk since mid-century.

Long-billed Curlew

Red Knot *Calidris canutus*

The Red Knot is found in Florida during migration and is quite common on the coasts where it feeds on sandy beaches. It is not often found in the interior of Florida at any season. The Red Knot can occasionally be found during the summer as well as winter but not in any great numbers. It does not breed in Florida and winters in South America but it can sporadically be found wintering on the Gulf Coast to Texas and the Atlantic coast as far north as Virginia and Maryland. Florida, as well as the entire southern coastline, is a good place to find the Red Knot in the fall as it feeds to fatten itself up for the nonstop flight across the Gulf to South America.

The Red Knot is most striking in its breeding plumage, a pale-rust color found especially on the breast. Its back is darker with a brownish-rust cast to it. The bird is short and compact at about ten inches tall. The bill is rather short, as is the neck.

The Red Knot resembles the Dowitchers in color and even feeds with them in loose flocks. But the Dowitchers have much longer bills, legs and necks and are overall a bit larger. Its winter plumage, which will be seen in Florida, is quite different than the rust-colored breeding plumage. The legs in both winter and breeding plumage are a gray-green. In winter, it is a clean-gray color overall with an almost white color on the underparts. Scalloping on the feather edges is quite faint, giving the overall, clean-gray look. In flight, faint wing lines are evident as well as the absence of the white rump of the Dowitcher.

The Red Knot was once one of the most abundant shorebirds found in North America. Even today, extremely large flocks can be found mixed with Dowitchers and other shorebirds as they migrate, especially during the fall.

The Red Knot was hunted extensively as many shorebirds were during the last half of the last century and has not fully recovered from that hunting. The sight of a few hundred to thousands of these birds in breeding plumage feeding on beaches or mud flats will not soon be forgotten.

The diet of the Red Knot consists of, for the most part, different mollusks found in mud flats and beaches. It will take aquatic insects, worms and horseshoe crab eggs. Being opportunistic it will not turn down any type of prey it finds while probing with its short bill on the beaches.

Red Knot
Winter plumage (top)

Willet *Catoptrophorus semipalmatus*

The Willet prefers the salty water of the coasts and is a common sight along the beaches of both coasts. It is more abundant during the winter when migratory birds move into the state from the west and north. The birds can be found in the interior of Florida with more frequency where there are shorelines of lakes and flooded fields. The Willet nests in the northern prairie states and the eastern United States coastline from Texas to Virginia. It spends the winters in the southern United States to South America. The Willet seems to be holding its own after being hunted extensively.

The Willet is a tall shorebird, standing nearly-a-foot-and-a-half tall. The bird when it is feeding is quite plain, being a mottled gray above with faint scaling on the light-gray underparts. The legs are long and blue-gray in color. The body is rather stocky, unlike the Yellowlegs with which it might be confused. The most striking feature of the Willet is the wing pattern exhibited when in flight. They have two heavy-black bands with a white band between them when the wing is outstretched. This is not exhibited at all when at rest. These black-and-white markings are quite prominent and no other shorebird of this size has these markings.

The call of the Willet during the breeding season is *pill will willet.* In flight the call is a *wee wee wee* in rapid succession.

The Willet places its nest near the wet areas it frequents where it hides it in thick vegetation. The nest is placed on the ground where grasses or sedges can conceal it. Nesting begins in Florida during the month of April and is usually complete by midsummer. One brood is produced per year. Being somewhat colonial, the nests of the Willet can be found grouped in a favorite area.

The nest is sparingly lined with vegetation in which four brown-marked, olive-colored eggs are laid. Incubation takes about four weeks. When the chicks hatch they are able to follow the parents soon after drying. The young may stay with the adults for over a month before the parents leave for other beaches and mud flats.

Feeding along beaches and mud flats the Willet takes advantage of whatever food it comes across. It readily takes mollusks, aquatic insects, crustaceans, worms, small fish and whatever else it can capture in the shallow waters of the shoreline. In flooded farm fields it takes advantage of the numerous insects available, especially grasshoppers and crickets.

Willet
Summer plumage (bottom)

Spotted Sandpiper *Actitis macularia*

One of the most common of the small sandpipers in the United States, the Spotted Sandpiper is a winter resident and fall and spring migrant in Florida. It is common in Florida along the wet margins of beaches, lakes, streams, marshes and swamps. It is common from August, when the first migrants return, through May when the last leave for the breeding grounds of North America (except the extreme northern part of Canada). A few Spotted Sandpipers may be seen during the summer, but are not common.

During the winter, the Spotted Sandpiper does not exhibit the spots that are its namesake, but are completely white underneath. The upper body is an olive-brown color with barring during the breeding season. A good winter characteristic to look for is the white spot in front of the wing "shoulder" made by the olive-color coming down from the neck to the front of the shoulder but not quite reaching it, leaving a white area. During the summer and breeding season, the front of the Spotted Sandpiper has pronounced black spots. An identifying characteristic of the Spotted Sandpiper it that it constantly bobs its tail, giving it the nick name "teeter tail." In flight, it flies stiffly in short bursts close to the water while often times giving its *peet weet weet weet* calls. Its legs are bright-yellow during breeding, but less bright during the winter. Except during migration, the Spotted Sandpiper is normally a solitary bird, found in ones or twos.

Spotted Sandpipers feed in a variety of ways and upon a variety of organisms. Most often the Spotted Sandpiper will be seen feeding along the waters edge of ponds, streams, marshes and swamps where it forages for all sorts of organisms from insects and crustaceans to small mollusks. It will also take small fish and worms. Often the Spotted Sandpiper can be seen wading in the water taking floating food from the surface. This behavior is especially apparent during the aftermath of a windy rainstorm when numerous organisms have been blown in the water and drowned. In the breeding range, as well as in Florida, the Spotted Sandpiper is able to capture flying insects from the air. In the north, we are accustomed to seeing this bird walking, feeding and teetering along the beaches and water's edge.

One reason the Spotted Sandpiper bird is so abundant is that it may have as many as five successful broods in a season. The female arrives on the breeding ground before males and selects the males. Males take care of the nest and young which is unusual in the bird world.

Spotted Sandpiper
Winter plumage (top)   Summer plumage (bottom)

Short-billed Dowitcher   *Limnodromus griseus*

A common shorebird of the fall and spring migration seasons, the Short-billed Dowitcher can be found during the winter months as well. It is an infrequent summer visitor but some are usually seen each summer. Populations of these birds are highest during the peak of migration, during April and August. The Short-billed Dowitcher usually migrates to South America for the winter but it can spend it in parts of the southern United States on both the Atlantic and Gulf coasts. During the winter they can be found from Virginia to Texas, in increasing numbers the further south you travel, although not found in any great numbers after the main thrust of migration. In Florida, they are found on wet shorelines of lakes, marshes and the coastline beaches. Occasionally in migration they will be found in flooded agricultural fields. The Short-billed Dowitcher nests in the tundra and bogs of Canada and Alaska.

In Florida, both the winter plumage as well as the breeding plumage can be seen. The winter plumage is the most common as the Short-billed Dowitcher is not a breeder of Florida and breeding plumage doesn't begin to arrive until migration is underway. At about a foot tall, the Short-billed Dowitcher's most recognizable feature is its extremely long bill. The winter plumage is predominately gray-and-white. The bottom of the bird is a white-gray with little markings. The upper part of the bird is brownish-gray to gray during the winter. The head has a white line above the eye and a dark stripe though the eye. The legs are a greenish-gray in color. Another pronounced feature is its white rump and light-gray tail that makes a wedge part of the way up the back.

Rarer than the Short-billed Dowitcher is the Long-billed Dowitcher, which is more heavily marked on the breast and has a slightly longer bill. The call of the Short-billed Dowitcher is a rapid three-note, flute-like *tu tu tu*, while the Long-billed Dowitcher's call is a loud, single call of *keek*.

The long bill of the Dowitcher allows it to probe in the wet sand and mud of the shorelines. Its diet is a variety of aquatic and land organisms. The Short-billed Dowitcher seems to prefer the saltwater beaches but is common on any type of water where it eats aquatic insects, crustaceans, mollusks and worms. The long bill is an aid in obtaining the worms and some of the insects and mollusks that burrow in the mud. The Dowitchers are good swimmers and may take some organisms from the water surface, but they prefer to probe.

Short-billed Dowitcher
Summer plumage (bottom)

Ruddy Turnstone *Arenaria interpres*

The Ruddy Turnstone frequents Florida mainly in migration but is also a common winter visiter. In winter the Ruddy Turnstone can be found on the coasts of North America and into the southern hemisphere. Few of these birds can be found in the interior of Florida after migration. Agricultural fields and freshwater areas will be used by these birds in migration, but birds staying the winter seem to prefer the coasts. The breeding grounds of the Ruddy Turnstone are the extreme coastlines of northern Canada, Greenland and Alaska above the Arctic Circle. It prefers to nest in tundra areas near the coastline.

The winter plumage of the Ruddy Turnstone is quite different than that of the striking breeding garb. The Turnstone is a small, chunky bird, standing about eight or nine inches tall. In winter it is brown above with a darker-brown bib or band across its upper chest with otherwise white underparts and white throat. The legs are an orange-yellow and are paler during the non-breeding season. The bill is rather short and stout at the base. The bill has a gentle upward curvature upward.

In flight, the black-and-white patterns of the wings and back make these birds unmistakable. The most obvious feature is the oval patch of white on the lower upper back and black bar across a white tail. During breeding the brown on the back becomes a golden-brown and the face and neck become strikingly black-and-white. The head has strong black-and-white markings, making the Ruddy Turnstone quite beautiful.

The Ruddy Turnstone gets its name from its rust-colored breeding plumage and because it uses its upturned bill to deftly turn over shoreline stones and debris to locate the critters hiding beneath including crustaceans, mollusks, worms, insects and whatever else it may find. It is extremely fond of Horseshoe Crab eggs and will dig down into the sand to find them. The Ruddy Turnstone is also known for stealing eggs from other bird's nests. It therefore likes to associate its nesting grounds with that of other small seabirds.

In Florida this bird is not afraid of humans and many people frequenting the beaches and fishing areas see the Ruddy Turnstone, even coming quite close to it before it flushes from a rock, deck or fishing pier.

Ruddy Turnstone
Summer plumage (top)

Dunlin *Calidris alpina*

In Florida, the Dunlin is primarily a winter resident and bird of the migration season. Rarely are these birds seen during the summer months. The first fall migrants arrive as early as late July and almost all have left by the end of May. The Dunlin is primarily a bird of the coastal wet areas and is found extensively on beaches, mud flats, tidal pools and estuary shorelines. During migration they may be found inland on freshwater shorelines and agricultural flooded fields, but once migration is complete they prefer the coastal waterways. The Dunlin's nesting grounds are, similar to the Ruddy Turnstones, the extreme coastlines of Alaska, Greenland and Canada. The Dunlin spends the winter on the North American coastline and in Central America and coastal Mexico.

For the most part, when the Dunlin is found in Florida it is a rather dull bird. It is a gray-brown color above with pale-gray breast and white underparts. Faint markings are found on the back and upper breast. A white eye-stripe is evident. The legs and bill are black. The bill of the Dunlin is noticeably down-turned at the tip. The bill is rather long and fairly thick. Faint wing stripes are evident in flight. In May the birds take on their breeding plumage of a rust-gold-colored back and a dark-black belly which is unmistakable. Occasionally, while wading in deeper water the black belly will be in the water and not seen. Not all the birds will have molted before leaving for the breeding grounds so you may see mixed flocks in various stages of molting. In fact, one identifying feature is that the Dunlin can be found in groups. The call of the Dunlin is a loud harsh *kreezt* given when taking flight or in flight. During migration the Dunlin can be one of the most numerous of Florida's sandpipers.

Their long bill makes the Dunlin adept at obtaining food from the soft mud and sand of the wet areas where it feeds. Its food consists of marine aquatic insects, mollusks, crustaceans, insects washed up on shore, worms and other invertebrates. Depending on their wintering sites, some Dunlins become quite adept at taking marine worms. Seeds will be eaten, especially during migration, primarily in agricultural fields, but being opportunistic they won't pass up any available food. This is markedly true during migration when energy is at a premium.

Dunlin
Summer plumage (bottom)

Common Snipe *Gallinago gallinago*

The Common Snipe, the object of pranks of many summer campers, is a winter resident of Florida and occurs from September through May. This bird does not breed in Florida and is most common in the northern part of the state during the winter. The Snipe is a bird of open wetlands and shorelines. In Florida they can be found in wet prairies, marshes, river and stream sides, as well as agricultural lands during migration. Although this bird can be found along the coast in brackish water, it is more common in habitats that have freshwater where it wades in the shallows searching for food. It is similar to the American Woodcock in its habitat requirements, although it is slimmer and the stripping on the head is across the head on the Woodcock.

The Common Snipe is less than a foot tall and has shorter legs than most shorebirds. It looks stockier and has an extremely long bill, appearing to be nearly half the length of the body. The legs are a greenish-yellow and short for a shorebird. It has marked patterns over the body which are more striking than most shorebirds. The head has lateral stripes running from the bill to the back of the head. It is brown overall with a light-colored belly, the markings being black or dark-brown. In flight the tail is a bright-rust color with black bars crossing it. A common characteristic is the extremely erratic flight that the bird uses when flushed. The snipe gives a sharp *skeet* or *creet* call as it zig-zags away. The Snipe and Woodcock both like to sit tight to try to avoid being discovered. Only at the last minute do they flush, usually startling us as they take off, literally at our feet. The Common Snipe is not found out in the open as often as many of the other shorebirds.

The diet of the Common Snipe is plants, seeds and aquatic organisms: crustaceans, worms, insects and mollusks. In migration it may be seen with other shorebirds feeding along the wet sand margins of lakes and rivers. But once it has established itself for the winter it tends to be more solitary, seeming quite shy, and preferring less open areas.

The Snipe breeds in the northern part of the United States and Canada in wet prairie and open habitats near wetlands. In Canada it nests in the tundra. In its breeding grounds it does a spectacular breeding display called "winnowing." The male flies high up into the air and then settles downward as he flutters his tail feathers which make a *whu whu whu whu whu* sound as he descends. This display usually occurs during the daytime hours and may occur while the birds are migrating.

Common Snipe

Sanderling *Calidris alba*

The Sanderling is probably the most recognized and most often seen of the beach sandpipers. It is a winter resident of Florida and exhibits different color patterns during the winter than the summer. Rarely will this bird be found in Florida during the summer, but occasionally Sanderlings can be seen along the coastal beaches. Only occasionally will the Sanderling be found inland and then usually only on the larger bodies of water where beaches are common.

The Sanderling is fairly common along all the southern coasts but nests in the extreme arctic tundra of Canada and Alaska. This little bird is circumpolar and is found in Europe as well as the United States. The Sanderling is found predominately on beaches where wave action stirs up the sandy margins uncovering food for them to eat: insects, tiny shellfish or sand fleas. During migration, the Sanderling may be found with other shorebirds in almost any wet area. Once a wintering territory has been successfully established the Sanderling will return year after year.

At about eight inches tall, the Sanderling is a predominately light-gray, almost white, bird with black legs. The underparts of the Sanderling are white. The bill is relatively short and black. In the winter the Sanderling exhibits a pronounced black shoulder-patch or stripe. In flight a white wing stripe is shown against a dark wing and the outer tail feathers show white.

In breeding plumage, which is rarely seen except for the summer months, the gray upper parts are replaced with a rich-brown or deep-tan color. Also, the breast becomes rust-colored and the white underparts become a light-buff. Immature birds that arrive in Florida are similar to the winter adults except they are more buff-colored above and not so gray.

Probably the most identifiable characteristic of these small birds is their feeding behavior. The birds gather in small groups of up to a dozen (but usually less), and follow the waves back and forth. When disturbed from the beach the Sanderling flies out over the water giving a *kip kip kip kip* call. But they return quickly to the water's edge just a short distance away.

In the tundra the Sanderling nests on the ground in a nest lined with soft grasses and leaves. Usually four brown-speckled, olive-colored eggs are laid and are incubated for about four weeks depending upon the temperature and weather. Occasionally two clutches are produced. Once the young are hatched they grow rapidly, fledging in about three weeks. The adult Sanderlings protect their young in much the same way as the Killdeer which feigns injury to lure potential danger away.

Sanderling
Winter plumage (top)

Laughing Gull and Bonaparte's Gulls

Larus atricilla and Larus philadelphia

Two black-headed gulls which frequent Florida coastlines are the Laughing Gull and Bonaparte's Gulls. The main difference between them is that the Laughing Gull nests in Florida, whereas the Bonaparte's Gull is only a winter resident.

In breeding plumage, both of these gulls have an entirely black head. However, the bill of the Laughing Gull is red-orange whereas the Bonaparte's Gull has a black bill. Also, the Laughing Gull has a dark-gray mantle and the Bonaparte's Gull a light-colored mantle. In winter, both gulls lose the black head and only the color of the mantle remains to distinguish them apart. The Bonaparte's Gull has a black spot directly behind the eye and the Laughing Gull has what appears to be a smudged area from the eye to the back of the head.

Both gulls are considered to be small- to medium-sized: the Laughing Gull at about sixteen inches and the Bonaparte's Gull at about thirteen inches. In flight, the Bonaparte's Gull can be identified by the extreme white leading edge of the wing, which is noticeable from great distances. Both of these gulls are common along both coasts of Florida in their seasons. Occasionally they will be found inland, but they prefer the coastline. The Laughing Gull has learned to adapt to the handouts of man and can be found inland more frequently than the Bonaparte's Gull.

The Laughing Gull gets its name from its call which is a loud raucous *ha ha ha ha*. It nests in Florida and all along the coast north to Cape Cod. The Laughing Gull is most abundant near the Tampa bay area. The Bonaparte's Gull nests in Canada, but winters all along the eastern coast of the United States. The Laughing Gull has become increasingly common and in some areas has become abundant.

Both gulls feed along the coasts on fish and other marine life. The Laughing Gull is more aggressive and will steal food from other gulls and terns. The Laughing Gull nests in the spring with nesting being nearly complete by the end of June.

Usually three to four dark-olive eggs marked with brown are laid on the ground in a shallow depression. The nest is usually well hidden by dune vegetation and is lined with grasses, small twigs and beach debris. The nests can be located in fairly large colonies, where added protection is afforded by sheer numbers.

The eggs are incubated by both parents for about three weeks. The young are fed partially-digested food while small but as they grow larger and older they will be able to take whole organisms. They leave the nest at about five weeks of age. As in most gulls, immature birds are hard to distinguish because it may take as long as four years for them to reach their mature breeding plumages.

Laughing Gull
Summer plumage, in flight (top left)
Winter, head (bottom, left)

Bonaparte's Gull
Summer plumage, in flight (top right)
Winter, head (bottom, right)

Herring Gull and Ring-billed Gull

Larus argentatus and Larus delawarensis

The Herring Gull and Ring-billed Gulls frequent most waterways, interior or coastal, of the United States. In Florida and along the coasts of the southern United States they are winter visitors. They nest in the Great Lakes region or further north and west. These birds can be a bit difficult to identify when seen individually, but with a little practice they can be identified with relative ease and assuredness.

Both gulls are relatively large, although the Herring Gull is the larger at two feet, compared to under twenty inches for the Ring-billed Gull. Both gulls have gray mantles with black wingtips and yellow bills. However, unlike the Ring-billed Gull, the Herring gull has a red spot on the lower mandible of its bill which some believe is a "feeding spot" that young Herring Gulls strike at to stimulate regurgitation so they can feed. The Ring-billed Gull has a black ring which completely encircles its bill near the tip. The legs and feet of these two birds are also different. The Herring Gull's feet and legs are flesh- to pink-colored, whereas the Ring-billed Gull's feet and legs are yellow. In the adult plumage of both birds the head and tail is snow-white. Immature birds of both species are a dull-gray overall and take several years to reach breeding plumage.

Both of these gulls are common and abundant winter residents in Florida as well as over much of the United States coastline. Arriving in early fall, they remain in Florida as late as May. Some immature birds remain along the coasts during the summer but normally all breeding birds will leave.

Traditionally, these gulls were primarily birds of the coastlines but because of their scavenging nature they have adapted well to the world of man and can be found throughout the state wherever there may be a free handout as, for instance, in landfill areas. They also have learned to beg for food and are numerous on public beaches. They even frequent the "Golden Arches" where they get handouts of french fries and Big Macs (hold the pickle)!

In Florida during the fall through spring season they are the most common and abundant of all the gulls. Of the two, the Ring-billed Gull is the most likely to be seen in the interior while the larger Herring Gull prefers the coastline.

Both of these species seem to be increasing in numbers and seem to be expanding their ranges. This population increase has caused some concern for the smaller seabirds, such as the terns, because the larger gulls prey upon them. The Herring and Ring-billed Gulls have been known to take the chicks of terns as well as the eggs and nestlings of many shorebirds.

Herring Gull
Head (middle center)

Ring-billed Gull
In flight (top) Head (left)

Royal Tern and Caspian Tern

Sterna maxima and Sterna caspia

Unlike the gulls, the Terns are very graceful in flight and appear more sleek and slender. The Terns have sharply-pointed bills which they use to capture fish as they dive into the water headfirst. Gulls will sit on the water, whereas the Terns are constantly in flight.

The Royal Tern and Caspian Tern are the two largest terns found in Florida, or even North America for that matter. Of the two, the Caspian Tern is the largest, reaching almost two feet with the Royal Tern around twenty inches. In breeding plumage they are quite handsome birds. Their bodies are predominantly white, with the heads having a strongly contrasting black "cap." The Royal Tern has a yellow-orange bill with a black crest on its head. Its tail is forked to nearly half its length and the wingtips don't show much gray. However, in the Caspian Tern there is quite a lot of gray at the wingtips. The Caspian Tern has a massive burnt-red bill which frequently has a black tip. Both terns have short, black legs and black feet.

Often these terns can be seen resting on sand bars or beaches all pointed in the same direction as if in formation. Although these birds are most common along the coasts, in recent years they have been found along inland lakes and waterways. Since these terns nest in Florida they can be found here throughout the entire year but winter migrants do increase the populations considerably in winter.

Although these Terns breed in Florida, the breeding populations were almost wiped out during the 1800s. Today there are substantial populations in Tampa Bay, Merritt Island National Wildlife Refuge and other areas. The total numbers seem to be increasing for both species. Although the colonies of these terns are not as large as others throughout the world, some Florida colonies may number one thousand.

The Royal Tern and Caspian Tern feed on fish, crustaceans and other small marine organisms. The terns hover before diving into the water to capture a fish or possibly a squid. Although they do steal food from other seabirds, this techniques it is not a primary food-gathering source.

Both of these Terns lay their eggs in nests placed on the ground. The Caspian Tern and Royal Tern normally have one buff-colored egg with brown blotches in the nest, but may occasionally have two. Incubation is about four weeks. In about three days, the Royal Tern chicks leave their parents and join a group, or creche, of fledglings that are guarded by a few unrelated adults. The adults find and feed the young in these groups. The group affords protection from predation. The young are able to leave the supervision of adults in five to six weeks.

Royal Tern
Early summer, in flight (top left)
Winter, head (bottom center left)

Caspian Tern
Summer plumage, in flight (top right)
Winter, head (bottom right)

Forster's Tern and Common Tern

Sterna forsteri and Sterna hirundo

Both the Forster's and Common Terns are medium-sized, being just fourteen inches or so long. They are primarily winter residents of Florida as well as fall and spring migrants. Some straggling birds may occasionally remain for the summer and limited nesting of the Common Tern has occurred in the panhandle of Florida.

The easiest way to distinguish between these two terns is the pattern of the primary feathers in their wings. In the Common Tern, the primary feathers are dark-gray; in the Forster's Tern the wings are white. The Forster's Tern also has a longer and more deeply-forked tail than the Common Tern. In winter plumage, which is most common in Florida, the Common Tern's black cap changes to a smaller black area from the eye around to the back of the head. The Forster's Tern's black cap changes to a black mask which does not go around to the back of the head. Both of these birds have an orange bill that is usually black-tipped.

The Common Tern is usually found in the offshore waters and is not common inland. In the ocean, it feeds upon small fish which it catches by diving into the water. The Forster's Tern can be found along the coasts as well as inland in freshwater areas, although it prefers the coastal waters. The Common Tern is not as abundant during the winter months as most of them migrate further south into Central and South America.

Both of these terns commonly breed in the northern parts of North American; the Forster's Tern in the west and the Common Tern in the northern United States and Canada. Both of these birds typically lay three buff-colored eggs with brown blotches which sometimes encircle the egg like a wreath. The nest of the Forster's Tern is more elaborate and is lined with grasses and aquatic vegetation. The Common Tern's nest is just a scrape in the sand that is sometimes lined with a few stones and pebbles. Incubation takes just over three weeks. Often the third egg hatched produces a weaker chick that may not survive. The young are able to leave the nest in about three to five weeks.

Both of these terns feed by diving into the water to catch small fish and other marine or freshwater organisms and insects. Forster's Terns even capture flying insects over inland waters. Both have somewhat learned to adapt to man, taking advantage of handouts from beaches and the wakes of fishing boat. Forster's Terns seems to have adapted more easily to man's presence, possibly because the Common Tern is more comfortable over the larger bodies of salt water.

Common Tern
Summer, in flight (top left)
Winter, Head (center bottom left)

Forster's Tern
Summer, in flight (second from top, right)
Winter, Head (bottom right)

Roseate Tern   *Sterna dougallii*

The Roseate Tern is both a breeding bird of Florida as well as a migratory bird from colonies of the North Atlantic coastline. In Florida, it is a breeding bird of the Dry Tortugas as well as the Keys (just within the last twenty years). Migration reports are mostly limited to the Atlantic coastline down which it is presumed that the birds from the United States and Canadian coastlines move for the winter. Very rarely is this bird found inland and then only after severe storms.

The Roseate Tern is another black-capped tern but, unlike the Forster's and Common Tern, it has a dark bill, which is entirely black in winter. During breeding, the base of the bill may be a dark-orange, appearing black from a distance. The last few primaries are black, but do not show as much as the Common Tern. Unlike the Common and Forster's Tern, while the Roseate is sitting on the ground, the long tail-forks extend significantly beyond the wingtips. In the other two terns the wingtips will be fairly near or at the end of the tip of the tail. In winter the head of the Roseate Tern will resemble that of the Common Tern except it will have a black bill. Location of these birds should help in identification, as they are uncommon out of their range.

Primarily fish-eaters, the Roseate Tern prefers to eat fish near shore. Though they may wander throughout the oceans they prefer to feeding near shore areas where large schools of small fish can be taken at ease. This tern may also feed upon small mollusks and other marine life and it is not above stealing food from other gulls or even terns when given a chance. Pelicans seem to attract terns who take advantage of them as they forage for food. When the Pelican comes up with a pouch full of fish and water, the terns will take whatever small fish escape as the water escapes. I have even seen terns sitting on the head and bill of the pelican waiting for a handout to come along from the pelican's mouth!

Nesting occurs on the ground with concealment by dune grass or some beach vegetation. Sometimes the nest will be placed upon bare rocks or in rocky places. In the Florida colonies the nests are very susceptible to flooding and extra-high tides, such as those from tropical storms and hurricanes. The nests can be lined with beach grasses and other herbaceous material. Two brown-marked, buff-colored eggs are incubated for about three-and-a-half weeks. The young can leave the nest in about four to five weeks but will continue to be fed for a few weeks longer. Both parents are in attendance during incubation and fledging.

Roseate Tern
Winter Head (left)   Summer Head (right)

Gull-billed Tern and Sandwich Tern

Sterna nilotica and Sterna sandvicensis

The Gull-billed Tern and Sandwich Terns are both black-capped terns of medium size. The Sandwich Tern is the larger of the two birds at about eighteen inches. Their heads are the feature that distinguishes these birds apart from the other terns. The Sandwich Tern has a black bill with a yellow tip in all plumages. In the breeding plumage, the black cap is crested in the back. The Gull-billed Tern has a solid, thick, black bill which, as its name implies, is more gull-like than tern-like. In the winter the Gull-billed Tern's head is almost white with a gray wash over the back part and nape. Both have black feet and show only a small amount of dark on the primary wing feathers when in flight.

Both birds nest in Florida. The Gull-billed Tern nests both inland and along the coasts, although not in any large colonies and with somewhat dubious regularity. The Gull-billed Tern is one of the most common inland nesting terns. Its nests are placed on smooth beaches, scrapes, gravel pits and even abandoned, bare fields. The nest is placed on the bare ground and ringed with various objects that are at hand. Two or three buff-colored eggs marked with brown splotches are incubated for just over three weeks. Both parents take care of incubation and the young. Fledging occurs in about five weeks.

The Gull-billed Tern, instead of diving for its food, hovers over it, then swoops down to grab it. The diet of this tern includes insects, small mammals, crustaceans, amphibians, spiders and occasionally reptiles. The Gull-billed Tern is comfortable in the agricultural areas of Florida. The Sandwich Tern dives for small fish, but it also eats small crustaceans, shrimp, insects and small squid.

The Sandwich Tern is limited in its nesting area to the Bird Islands in Nassau Sound. Development and loss of beach property has contributed to the decline of nesting areas. Usually two buff-colored eggs with dark-brown markings are laid in a nest on open sandy beaches. Little or no nest preparation is done. Incubation is shared for about three-and-a-half weeks and both parents take care of the chicks until they leave at about five weeks.

Sandwich Tern chicks, after three or four days, join a creche with other chicks until they fledge. The parents are able to pick their chick out of all the rest of the chicks in the creche by its call. The creche is usually composed of both Sandwich and Royal Tern chicks. These terns will associate with each other as adults and even return to nesting areas together. However, the Sandwich Tern, unlike the Gull-billed Tern, is a coastal bird and is infrequent inland.

Gull-billed Tern
Summer, in flight (second from top, right)
Winter, Head (bottom right)

Sandwich Tern
Summer, in flight (top left)
Winter, Head (center bottom left)

Black Skimmer   *Rynchops niger*

The Black Skimmer is a coastal bird that can be found along all of Florida's coastlines. Dependant for its food on small fish swimming near the surface it is never far from water. It can be found on larger inland waters and occasionally on flooded fields. In Florida, it nests over the entire state except in the extreme south and Keys. Along the coasts it is common and is often associated with terns. Usually it is seen skimming the water, as its name implies, or sitting on sandbars with terns and gulls. It is also quite common along the Gulf coastline to Texas and into Mexico.

The name "Black Skimmer" comes from the fact that it is black on the back and "skims" the water for small fish. This feeding characteristic is enabled by its strange bill, which is long and pointed with the lower mandible nearly a third longer than the upper mandible. The bill is flat vertically which helps it glide through the water. The Black Skimmer catches fish by flying just above the water with its lower bill just cutting the surface. When the Skimmer locates a fish by feel, a quick snap of the bill captures the meal and, in this unique way, it picks up fish, shrimp and other aquatic organisms.

The Black Skimmer is quite striking with a black back and crown and white face and bottom. Its bill is bright-red with a black tip and the legs are red as well. Immature and winter birds are not as dark above but still retain the basic color pattern. In flight, the tail has a black streak down the center with white outer feathers.

The Black Skimmer nests on coastal beaches and sandbars. The nests are placed in shallow scrapes among shells and rocks. Nesting has come under increased pressure with the advance of coastal development and any human disturbance can greatly influence it. However, graveled rooftops have begun to provide an additional area for Black Skimmer nest.

Four or five pale buff-colored eggs marked with dark brown blotches are laid. The buff-color ranges from green and white to pink. Both sexes incubate the nest but it appears that the male is dominate in this process. The female has the role of protector, vigorously defending the nest and young. The eggs hatch in about three weeks, and three-and-a-half weeks are needed for the young to be able to leave the nest. While small the young are fed regurgitated fish but as they become older they will be able to take whole fish. The lower mandible is not longer at hatching and stays the shorter length until the birds have almost reached adult size. Juvenile birds hide themselves by covering themselves with sand in order to protect themselves from predators.

Black Skimmer

Common Ground Dove   *Columbina passerina*

The Common Ground Dove is only about six or so inches long, about half the size of the Mourning Dove. The Mourning Dove is quite common throughout the United States but the Ground Dove is limited to Florida and the southern coastal states to Texas and into parts of Arizona and New Mexico. Northward their range extends only into the Carolinas.

The Common Ground Dove is the smallest dove in the United States and is quite compact, with a comparatively shorter tail than the rest of the doves. In flight, it is most recognizable by the bright rust-colored primary wing feathers. The feathers on the head and chest have scalloped markings which give the bird a scaled effect. The male bird is a little more striking than the uniformly gray female. The underparts of the male give off a slight pinkish tinge and the back is a somewhat darker-brown. The legs and feet are yellow.

In Florida and much of the southeast the Common Ground Dove is declining in numbers. It is most common in rural areas and vacant feral areas around suburbia. It most often can be seen feeding on seeds in old fields and pastures. Although they will eat berries and some insects, seeds are the primary food of the Common Ground Dove. After harvest season it can be found with other doves foraging in old grain fields. As they are almost sparrow-sized they can be overlooked when feeding on the ground and be quite startling when flushed. As they fly the chestnut wings are quite evident.

In Florida, up to four broods can be raised as the Common Ground Dove as they nest at almost any time of the year. Two white eggs are laid in a rather loosely constructed nest of twigs in small trees or shrubs. The inner nest will contain some smaller and finer plant material. Occasionally they will reuse their nest or use that of another bird. Incubation is done by both parents for about two weeks. The young are attended by both parents and fed regurgitated food called "bird milk" or "crop milk." The young birds or "squabs," as they are called when feeding on the crop milk, will be able to leave the nest in just under two weeks. They will follow the parents around for a few days begging for food until they are on their own.

The Common Groud Dove's call is a soft cooing similar to that of the Mourning Dove except it is not as pronounced with a little inflection at the end.

Common Ground Dove

Mourning Dove *Zenaida macroura*

The Mourning Dove is the most common dove or "pigeon" in the United States. Although not striking in appearance nevertheless this bird is quite handsome. Sometimes called "Pinheads," the Mourning Dove has a small head which is characteristic of the family of pigeons and doves. Their overall color is a soft coffee-brown with black spots on the wings. The neck is an iridescent pattern of metallic colors. The head has an elongated black spot below the eye. The pointed tail is longer than that of other doves and pigeons and has pronounced white and black spots along the end of the tail feathers. When flying, the wings makes a whispering whistle sound and the flapping is quite loud when startled into flight. The overall length of the Slender Mourning Dove is about a foot.

This bird is found throughout Florida and the populations are greatly increased with migratory birds from the north during the winter. In many states as well as Florida the Mourning Dove is hunted for sport and meat. Some of the northern states do not allow this bird to be hunted as it is quite a popular bird at feeding stations. It is not known whether the name, Mourning Dove, comes from the plaintive call or because the call is quite evident during early dawn hours. Either way the call is a familiar *caooh oooh oooh oooh.*

Nests are placed in trees or shrubs, usually not over ten feet above the ground. The nest is constructed of twigs loosely erected in a shallow platform. Occasionally finer plant material may line the nest. Male birds provide the material for the nest while the female constructs it.

Normally two white eggs are laid in the nest and incubation is about two weeks. As in the Common Ground Dove, the young are fed crop milk and are able to leave the nest in about another two weeks. The Mourning Dove probably receives the award for the most broods produced during a year, sometimes up to six. In Florida and the southeast the nesting season is all year. Even in the north nesting may begin as the snow is leaving.

The diet of the Mourning Dove is grains and seeds. Most commonly you will see these pretty birds feeding in flocks on the ground, usually in open areas. During the winter, the huge flocks may feed together with the winter migrants. The range of the Mourning Dove seems to be expanding, possibly due to the popularity of birdfeeding stations and habitat created for birds.

Mourning Dove

Yellow-billed Cuckoo   *Coccyzus americanus*

Of the three Cuckoos found in the United States, the Yellow-billed Cuckoo is the most likely to be seen in Florida. The Black-billed Cuckoo is not found here and the Mangrove Cuckoo is rare. In Florida, as well as much of the eastern United States, the Yellow-billed Cuckoo is a summer resident, nesting in the United States but wintering in Central and South America.

A rather long bird at about a foot in length, the Yellow-billed Cuckoo has, as its name implies, a yellow bill. It is brown above with a white underside. The relatively long tail has bold white spots accented by a black background. In flight, the Yellow-billed Cuckoo's wings show rich mahogany or brownish-red patches in the wings similar to the Common Ground Dove. These rust-colored patches are absent in the other two Cuckoos. The Mangrove Cuckoo is similar except its undersides exhibit some buff coloration.

All the Cuckoos that nest in the United States have a slightly downcurved bill. Occasionally, but rarely, the Black-billed Cuckoo can be seen during migration. In Florida, the Yellow-billed Cuckoo is found throughout the state as well as much of the south. It is usually found in forest edges and open woodlands and is most often identified by its call. The call is a successive quick *kow kow kow* or *kuk kuk kuk* that finishes with a *kup*

or *kaup kaup*. In some areas this call is thought to be the precursor to rain and so the bird is often times called a "Rain Crow."

The nest of the Yellow-billed Cuckoo is usually in a deciduous shrub or small tree. The nest is a loose platform of twigs lined with grasses and smaller plant material including pine needles, bits of leaves, moss and lichens.

Three to four (or rarely six) pale-greenish eggs are incubated for just under two weeks by both parents. The young are fed a diet of protein-rich insects and grow rapidly, leaving the nest in less than two weeks, many times in less than ten days although they are attended by parent birds for a few weeks longer, first by the male and then by the female.

The diet of these relatively large birds is quite varied. They will feed on small reptiles and amphibians as well as a complete host of insects. Probably the biggest benefit of the Cuckoo is that it penetrates the nests of tent caterpillars and devours these insect scourges. The Yellow-billed Cuckoo eats fruit and berries in season but grain is not a high priority.

In Florida as well as much of the United States, the populations of this bird, as well as the other Cuckoos, have been declining and they are a species of concern.

Yellow-billed Cuckoo

Smooth-billed Ani *Crotophaga ani*

A rather large bird, the Smooth-billed Ani is limited to the southern half of Florida although on rare occasions it is found in northern Florida and straggling into the Carolinas. But, in general, the northern extent of the Smooth-billed Ani rarely extends further north than an east/west line extended from Tampa across the state. The range of this bird seems to have stabilized in the lower half of Florida although its actual population seems to be decreasing.

At over a foot in length, this jet-black bird is most easily recognized by its huge, almost deformed-looking bill and the long, disproportionally-sized, flopping tail. The bill of the Smooth-billed Ani has been compared to a that of the parrot but with no hook at the end. The tail, in flight, seems almost as if it is broken and is controlling the bird instead of the reverse. This tropical bird can be associated with flocks of Grackles and Cowbirds in agricultural areas. It seems to have established itself well to human-influenced habitats such as parks, old pasture lands, scrubby fields and parkland.

The Smooth-billed Ani nests in trees and shrubs about twenty-five feet tall, the nest itself is usually over six feet above the ground. The nest is quite large, constructed of a mass of twigs and lined only with leaves. The nests are made as a communal project and used for incubation as a shared or communal nest. More than one pair of birds will aid in the construction, lay their eggs and share incubation duties. Because of this cooperation the nest may contain as many as two dozen eggs depending upon the number of females using it. Each female will herself only lay about five or six eggs.

Nesting normally begins in March and continues through the early fall, although they may seize any opportunity that comes along during any time of the year. All the individuals of the cooperating group help in all aspects of the rearing process. Since new leaves are added to the nest as eggs are being laid, some are covered up with leaves and hatch at different intervals. The young of these birds fledge quite quickly, usually in a week, and the next layer of eggs will be incubated. It is not known whether this phenomenon is intentional or just circumstance.

Being a large bird at thirteen or fourteen inches long they are quite adept at capturing small lizards as well as many insects. They are omnivorous and are able to eat almost anything that comes their way but insects and small lizards make up most of their diet.

Smooth-billed Ani

Barred Owl *Strix varia*

The Barred Owl is found throughout Florida in mainland forests. This woodland owl doesn't like human habitation but in recent years has come to frequent edge communities near fairly large, intact woodlands. Sometimes called the "Swamp Owl," the Barred Owl is often found in the cypress and gum swamps of the south. This owl is fairly large at nearly two feet, with the male being somewhat smaller (as is typical among many raptors), but the Barred Owl is lighter than the similar-sized Great Horned Owl. The Barred Owl has dark-brown eyes and no ear tufts. It is a dark-brown overall with barring across the upper chest and vertical streaks on the belly. The brown coloration may vary dramatically from one bird to another. The bill of the Barred Owl is yellow and the facial disc is emphasized with a heavy dark ring around it.

The Barred Owl is the most easily seen owl in Florida. In many of the states parks and preserves like the Corkscrew Swamp Sanctuary, it can be found during the day sitting quietly in a tree. While walking the boardwalks through the swamp forests, look up into the trees or listen for the call of the Barred Owl bird. It is the most likely owl to call during the day and will come to investigate the call of any interloper. The Barred Owl will respond to a tape recording of their call as well as human imitations, which can easily be learned.

They are sometimes called "Hoot Owl," but really don't give the hoot that the Great Horned Owl does. Instead, the call of the Barred Owl goes *who cooks for you, who cooks for you all*. Often, when irritated, they will give off a *whoo ahh* and upon meeting another owl will do a number of strange calls, sometimes called "caterwauling," which sounds somewhat like chimpanzees calling back and forth. When attempting to call this or any bird be sure to check local restrictions. Never play a tape during the nesting season.

Nesting occurs in a tree hollow or stump, occasionally in a palm tree. In early winter, three white eggs are laid in the nest, which is lined with soft plant material and down. Four to five weeks of incubation are required for the eggs to hatch. Incubation begins with the first egg, so the young are hatched over several days.

The diet of the Barred Owl is extremely varied and includes rodents, small birds, crayfish, frogs and other reptiles and amphibians. During the summer months, insects can be a substantial part of the diet. Barred Owls will even make a meal of the tiny Screech Owl if given a chance.

Often associated with the Red-shouldered Hawk, the Barred Owls may share the same habitat on many occasions. They may even share their nests from year to year.

Barred Owl

Great Horned Owl *Bubo virginianus*

The most common large owl found in North America, the Great Horned Owl is also the most ferocious, so much so that it is sometimes called the "Flying Tiger." Another name for the Great Horned Owl is "Hoot Owl" because of the "hooting" call that it gives. The Great Horned Owl's call is a loud *whoo who-who who-who whoo* that can sometimes be heard over a mile away. Young owls, as they beg for food from the parents, will give a loud raspy screech, which can also be heard for a great distance.

The adult birds are about two feet tall and have a wingspan of five feet. Feathers arising from the top of their head give the appearance of ears or horns, although they are not. The eyes are yellow with black centers. The overall color is a heavily-barred brown becoming darker on the back. The facial disc is tan and a white throat patch is evident.

The Great Horned Owl can be found in a variety of habitats including barns. Their preferred habitat is open woodland and adjacent fields but the Great Horned Owl has also been found in swamps, river bottoms, city parks and palm plantations. The Great Horned Owl can be found throughout Florida.

The Great Horned Owl feeds on rabbits, squirrels and opossums; its favorite food is the slow-moving skunk (it appears to be impervious to its scent). When someone exclaims that they smell a skunk, more often than not what they are truly smelling is a victorious Great Horned Owl.

This bird builds its nests in a variety of places: hollow trees, abandoned hawk nests and tall stumps. In Florida, it may begin nesting as early as November and even in the far north it may begin while snow is still on the ground. Usually two white eggs are laid in the nest although sometimes three can be laid in years of good prey. Incubation is normally four weeks but may extend longer if weather is cool.

The young become "limbers" at about five to eight weeks after hatching. This means they can almost fly and usually leave the nest to go from limb to limb using their feet, beak and wings. It is at this time many find the young on the ground and assume they are orphaned—when nothing could be further from the truth. Even though they have left the nest, they are still be dependant upon the parents for several more months. This is the time when the young are most vocal, begging for food as they fly about their territory.

It has been reported that these owls may live for more than forty years if they make it through the first year. As with most owls the female is significantly larger than the male which permits less competition for sources of food. The larger female owl takes the larger prey while the male takes mice and smaller prey.

Great Horned Owl

Eastern Screech Owl *Otus asio*

The Eastern Screech Owl resembles a tiny Great Horned Owl and has many of same characteristics—except that it only reaches about eight inches in height. The Eastern Screech Owl is found throughout Florida and although it is not very common in the lower Keys, it is more frequent in the northern Keys. The habitat requirements of the Eastern Screech Owl are very diverse. Feeding can occur anywhere there are insects and mice along with some sort of perch. Nesting habitats are in areas where trees and cavities are available and it is for this reason that it is said they may be found "where six trees are together."

In Florida the Eastern Screech Owl has three color phases. The most common is a brown color, but the gray and red phase are not uncommon. In fact, all three of the color phases may exist in one brood. Like the Great Horned Owl these little owls have "horns" or ear-tuft feathers on their heads and heavily-streaked bodies in all color phases. Their eyes are yellow with black centers.

The call of the Eastern Screech Owl is quite distinct and unforgettable. There are two types: one a quivering whinny that may stay at the same pitch or may descend and the other a soft tremulo or trill that also wavers but remains pretty much monotone. Usually the trill is soft, but either call can be soft as well, leading you to believe that the bird may be a good distance away when it may well be directly overhead.

The Eastern Screech Owl can be called with a tape or an easily-learned whistle. They may not come as easily during the day as does the Barred Owl, but at night it will almost always respond readily. Since both Great Horned Owls and Barred Owls will readily eat Screech Owls, don't be surprised if either of these owls fly up to the tape player looking for a free meal.

In many parts of the country, people are putting up nest boxes for owls. In Florida, nesting begins in March when four or five white eggs are laid. The nest cavity is usually devoid of lining material except a few feathers and debris from prey. About four weeks are required to incubate the eggs and another four weeks before the young will fledge. Young owls will remain in the same tree or nearby for a week or more begging to be fed by the adults.

The diet of the Eastern Screech Owl is predominately insects but mice are also important to them. During the spring, immature birds of other species become a food source. As the summer progresses, large grasshoppers, katydids and crickets enter their diet. In some areas, the Eastern Screech Owl has wreaked havoc in the chipmunk and flying squirrel populations.

Eastern Screech Owl

Burrowing Owl   *Athene cunicularia*

As its name implies, this little owl lives in burrows in the ground. It is unique to Florida and the western United States where it is found over much of the prairie land. In Florida it was common in the prairie lands of the interior but the populations have decreased signification due to farming and development. The Burrowing Owl has learned to build colonies in vacant lots, golf courses, parks, pastures, airports and schools. Some communities have taken small colonies under their wing, so to speak, and keep vacant areas out of development for these little owls. With their adaptation to these new areas the populations of Burrowing Owls are on the comeback and even seem to be expanding northward. However, these birds are still not common in the Keys or in the extreme northern panhandle. During the fall, and occasionally the spring, vagrants arrive in Florida from as far north as Michigan and Maine.

The Burrowing Owl stands about ten inches tall and seems to be mostly leg. Their overall color is a light chocolate-brown with a mixture of bars and spots. The face has distinct white and black chin markings and it has small white spots on the top of the head. The eyes are yellow. Immature birds lack the heavy spotting on the breast. It is most often seen standing on small mounds of dirt at the entrance to the burrow, bobbing its head to gain depth perception. This quirk gives it the name "Howdy Owl," as if it is bobbing a hello.

Normally found in vacant fields, these little owls can be seen using fence posts, both day and night, to survey the area. Feeding is done predominantly at night but if young are present, then in the day as well. When disturbed these little owls will give a series of *clacks* or *chacks*. During the night or dusk hours it will also give a soft cooing similar to that of a Mourning Dove except it is higher-pitched. When the nest burrow is threatened the adults imitate a rattlesnake rattle to discourage would-be predators.

The nest burrow is most often a mammal-made burrow, usually that of a squirrel or prairie dog. Their nest is lined with materials at hand, from cow manure to their own feathers. The burrow extends at an angle and is from four to eight feet long with an enlarged nest cavity at the end.

In Florida, five to six eggs are common. The eggs are white but become quite dirty from the nest burrow. Incubation is done mostly by the female and takes three to four weeks with the young fledging in about four weeks. They will remain together as a family for several more months. Nesting is usually complete by mid-summer. Only one brood is raised during a year.

Burrowing Owl

Chuck-will's-widow   *Caprimulgus carolinensis*

The Chuck-will's-widow and Common Nighthawk belong to the family of birds called the "Nightjars" or "Goatsuckers." They are characterized by extremely large gapes for their soft, small bills (two inches for the Chuck-will's-widow). They capture insects in mid-air in their large, open mouths.

At nearly a foot long, the Chuck-will's-widow is the largest of the Nightjars. It is a well-camouflaged, soft-brown color overall. In flight, both the wings and tail are rounded at the tips. The tail is proportionately longer for the Chuck-will's-widow than for the Nighthawk. The throat is buff-colored with a white stripe below which sets off the dark breast. A close look will reveal the male has white in the outer tail feathers which are lacking in the female.

Location and voice are the best way to identify these birds. As its name implies, the call of the Chuck-will's-widow is a sharp and loud *chuck-will's-widow*. Unless you are relatively close sometimes the *chuck* is difficult to hear. They call during the evening, morning and nighttime hours either in flight, when sitting on the resting perch it uses to sleep on during the day or from seldom-used roadways. A good place to see and hear these birds is in the Florida state parks. If you drive slowly, you can hear them calling and may see their tell-tale red eyes in the glow of the headlights. During the day, the Chuck-will's-widow sleeps on the ground, a horizontal branch or fence rail, and leaves its resting place to feed at night. Often it will return to the same roost day after day, and even year after year.

In Florida, the Chuck-will's-widow is a year-round resident that breeds in the state. It is predominately an eastern bird, ranging from the Texas coast to the mid-Atlantic states and north to the southern Great Lakes. But only Texas, Louisiana and Florida have these birds the entire year. Even so, most will leave to winter in South and Central America.

The nests are made in a slight depression in the leaves of the forest floor in April. Two well-camouflaged eggs are incubated by the female for about three weeks. The young are able to help themselves soon after hatching and can hide themselves. The female takes care of the young for about two-and-half weeks before they are able to leave on their own. Only one brood is produced a year.

The diet of the Chuck-will's-widow is predominately insects, especially large beetles and moths. The large gape (mouth) is lined around the edge with long, stiff bristles to help guide insects into the mouth. It has been known to take small birds while in flight, swallowing them whole. Like owls, the flight of these birds is quite silent.

158

Chuck-will's-widow

Common Nighthawk *Chordeiles minor*

Probably the most recognized member of the Nighthawks is the Common Nighthawk. Its wings are pointed like a hawk and since it flies at night what better name to give it than "Nighthawk"? In Florida, it is a summer resident where it nests but spends the winter in South America. It arrives in Florida during March and nests by April. By late September it has left for the south. This bird prefers semi-open areas: pastures, agricultural fields and grasslands. It also has adapted to urban areas extremely well and is especially attracted to lakes and waterways.

The Common Nighthawk makes, a loud, harsh *peeent* as it flies over catching insects as well as a loud "*boom*" when the male dives downward to attract the female. In flight, across the primary feathers of the Common Nighthawk's wing, a pronounced white bar is evident and the throat exhibits a white patch. The wings are long and pointed and the tail is long with a slight notch. Male birds also show a white band across the end of the notched tail. The overall color is a brown-gray with camouflage markings. This color combination makes the Nighthawk almost impossible to see on the ground where it roosts and nests.

Although it feeds mainly at night, the Common Nighthawk can often be seen during the day. It is a common night visitor at shopping malls where it can be seen diving around the street and parking lights where insects gather. It is also found near waterways where dobsonflies and mayflies are leaving the water and taking to the air. Like the other Goatsuckers, the Common Nighthawk dives after insects with its huge, gaping mouth and captures them with the aid of the stiff bristles at the side of its mouth.

Nesting normally occurs on the ground, usually in a well-drained, open areas but it has also learned to put its nest on the flat, gravel roofs of large buildings. No real nest is made; at most a slight depression is used. The eggs are heavily-camouflaged in earth tones with a fine mottling that makes them appear like the leaves or the stones upon which they are resting. Two eggs are laid and are incubated for about two-and-a-half weeks.

The young are fed regurgitated insects and fledge in about three weeks. Young birds are lighter in color than adults. As September arrives most of the birds migrate south although a few stragglers or migrants may remain as late as November. In migration, you may see great numbers of these birds flying together, many times stopping as a group and taking advantage of insects coming off a lake or sewage pond. Occasionally they may be associated with groups of swallows during migration.

Common Nighthawk

Belted Kingfisher *Ceryle alcyon*

The waterways of Florida are home to the Belted Kingfisher where it can be found feeding on aquatic life, diving from a wire or perch at the water's edge. Although the Kingfisher is a permanent resident of Florida, the populations are varied and change with the seasons. Because they nest on the banks or river and streams, southern Florida is not preferred as a breeding area. Northern Florida and the panhandle have a greater number of kingfishers during the summer breeding season because of the greater topography variations. Winter populations are scattered throughout the state and this is when they are most common.

The Belted Kingfisher is a fairly large bird at just over a foot tall. It is stocky and the large, pointed bill makes it appear even larger. The Kingfisher is slate-blue with a crested head which makes it seem much larger. Both sexes have a white band around the neck and white undersides and a white patch in front of the eye just above the base of the bill. The female has a large, rust-colored band across her belly. The bill is black, strong, long and pointed, making it extremely efficient for catching fish. The legs and feet of the Kingfisher are short and small but they are strong, as they use them to scrape out a hole in a bank to make a nest.

Kingfishers hunt fish by diving into the water headfirst. It then goes back to its perch and swallows it headfirst. Although preferring fish, the Kingfisher will eat a variety of aquatic organisms: amphibians, squid, reptiles, insects, small mammals and baby birds. Like owls they will regurgitate a pellet of undigestible material.

Nests are placed in holes in a bank or bluff. Often these are along rivers but may be in gravel pits or waste piles. The average tunnel is about six feet deep and sometimes slants upward to avoid flooding. The nest chamber is lined with grass and leaves. It may take the pair of birds as much as three weeks to dig a tunnel, with both birds alternating in doing the scraping. Successful tunnels may be use repeatedly over the years. You can tell the entrance of a Kingfisher tunnel from those of other animals by the two grooves made where the feet hit at the entrance.

Five to seven pure-white eggs are laid and incubation is shared for three-and-a-half weeks. Depending upon the food supply, the young may fledge in as little as three weeks, often taking longer. Once the young leave the nest the adults will teach them to feed by dropping dead fish in the water and having the new fledglings dive for them. Usually in less than two weeks the young are adept enough that the adults drive them from their feeding territory.

Belted Kingfisher

Ruby-throated Hummingbird *Archilochus colubris*

The Ruby-throated Hummingbird is the smallest hummingbird and is common in Florida where it is a permanent resident. The greatest influx of these birds occurs during from March through May and August through October. Some Ruby-throated Hummingbirds will remain all winter in parts of Florida but most migrate to Central and South America. While in Florida they add a full third to their weight, enough to carry them across the Gulf of Mexico.

The Ruby-throated Hummingbird is easy to identify; its back is an iridescent metallic-green and its underparts white. The male has a bright-red throat, called a "gorget." Females and immature birds are just white under the throat. The female has a squared-off tail with white spots and the male has a forked tail with no spots. Both sexes have a white spot behind the eye.

Weighing less than a penny, these tiny birds are the only birds that can fly backward as well as upside down. They hover easily while their long, needle-like bill probes in flowers for their favorite food, nectar, or perhaps a small insect. Red and orange flowers seem to attract these birds better than other flowers. Even though red flowers are preferred I have seen these little guys visit the white flowers of blueberry and the greenish flowers of the Solomon's Seal. It's also fun to watch them take small gnats and other flying insects from the air and spiders from the "balloon webs" that carry the babies away from the egg capsule.

Nesting begins in May and is complete by mid-summer. The female is the sole builder of the nest and incubates and feeds of the young as well. The nest is built of spider silk, lichens and moss and lined with plant down, commonly that of willow or cottonwood. The nest is usually placed in a tree that is not too far from water, on a branch that angles downward and generally near a small fork. The nest can be placed as close to the ground as six feet, but I have also seen them as much as fifty feet from the ground.

Two extremely small white eggs are laid and incubated for about two weeks. The female feeds the young a mixture of nectar and high-protein insects. Depending upon the availability of food and the temperature, fledging may occur in as little as two weeks or take twice that long. Young birds don't have long bills until nearly ready to fledge. Two broods are common.

Hummingbirds seem to be increasing in some areas, possibly due to the increase of feeding. Many people are planting gardens specifically to attract hummingbirds as well as placing feeders out for them. It is important to put the feeder in exactly the same location at the beginning of the season as the hummingbird will always return to the last spot the feeder was located.

Ruby-throated Hummingbird

Chimney Swift *Chaetura pelagica*

In Florida there is only one type of Swift—the Chimney Swift. This bird is a small, dark and fast-flying. They can be seen during the day flying high in the sky hunting insects. Their wings are pointed and their body is short and cigar-shaped. In fact, the Chimney Swift has been called the "Flying Cigar."

The Chimney Swift appears almost tailless with the portion of the body in front of the wings almost equal to that behind the wings. The underside is a little lighter but it is not noticeable except upon close viewing. The tail is unforked. In flight, the Chimney Swift gives off a constant chattering especially when approaching the nesting chimney.

In Florida, this bird is a common migrant and summer resident. Although not extremely common during the nesting period, it is becoming more common around human habitations. It arrives in Florida from South America during March and begins nesting in April. As a cavity nester, it commonly nests in hollow trees, caves and caverns. Today, it nests in chimneys and wells as well. A crescent-shaped nest is built of twigs which are glued together with powerful saliva to the inner side of a chimney wall. It may take as long as a month for the nest to be completed, and even then it doesn't appear very substantial.

Four to five white eggs are laid on the small platform and incubated by both parents for about three weeks. Usually the nest is placed a good distance down the chimney, almost to the bottom on a residential home chimney and twenty feet or more into commercial chimneys. Often nesting is communal and additional non-breeding birds may assist in the care of young and even incubation.

The young will remain in the nest for up to a month, becoming quite loud during the last couple of weeks. Prior to leaving the chimney the young are able to crawl about with sharp claws. If the temperature gets too hot in the chimney the adult birds will fly into the chimney and hover, creating a fan for the young which passes air over them and the nest. They can keep this up for fairly long periods. Post-breeding populations can produce quite large flocks that roost together in some of the larger chimneys. By the end of October the Chimney Swift has left Florida for South America.

The Chimney Swifts are related to the Hummingbirds in that they have very small feet and short legs. Their wing beats are very rapid and they almost never land on any flat horizontal surface. The Swift's feet are very short and most of their time is spent in the air. Some people have even said that they don't ever land.

Chimney Swift

Pileated Woodpecker   *Dryocopus pileatus*

The Pileated Woodpecker is normally found in large wooded areas and is not commonly found in urban areas. However, it is becoming more common in the southeast as it adapts to the woodlots and other urban habitats. The Pileated Woodpecker is absent in the lower Keys and not extremely common in the northern Keys. Probably the best place to find the Pileated Woodpecker is in man-made parks and preserves. In these areas this otherwise shy bird can be readily seen and approached.

In addition to its large size, this woodpecker is easy to identify by its flaming-red crest. The cartoon character, Woody Woodpecker, is probably modeled after the Pileated Woodpecker. Both sexes have the crests, but the female's forehead is black instead of red. The faces of both are patterned with black-and-white with the male having a red bar extending like a moustache from the base of the bill. The bodies are predominantly black but show a great amount of white on the underwings when in flight, especially from the front. The call is a loud resounding *wucka wucka wucka*, similar to the Common Flicker, only it is more emphatic and irregular.

Another identifying characteristic of the Pileated Woodpecker is the rectangular shape and depth (some are several inches deep) of the cavities it excavates in search of wood-boring beetles and carpenter ants.

Courtship begins in late winter with the male calling to the female, raising its crest, and bobbing its head back and forth. He may open his wings and circle the tree while bobbing. Upon pairing, a joint flight may occur with the male circling the female. Usually four or five white eggs are laid in a nest cavity with incubation taking about two-and-a-half weeks. The young are fed regurgitated food and leave the nest in about four weeks. However, they may remain with the parents for awhile with both taking care of them.

Typically this large woodpecker needs large expanses of woodlots to thrive but since man has eliminated these large, forested tracts, the Pileated Woodpecker has learned to adapt to smaller woodlots and urban areas. Many times it flies nearly a mile between woodlots searching for food and looking for a nest site.

Although the normal diet of the Pileated Woodpecker is carpenter ants and beetles it will readily take nuts and berries in season. Not only will it tap into standing trees but it takes apart stumps and logs for some insects. Occasionally they will take insects from the ground as does the Common Flicker. They can be readily attracted with suet to a birdfeeding station.

Pileated Woodpecker

Northern Flicker *Colaptes auratus*

The Northern Flicker is also called the Yellow-shafted Flicker and is one of the only woodpeckers that commonly feeds upon the ground on ants and other insects. Three types of flickers have been combined to become the Northern Flicker: the Yellow-shafted, Red-shafted and the Gilded Flicker. In the eastern United States and Florida, the Yellow-shafted Flicker is the one that breeds.

The Northern Flicker is a large woodpecker at over a foot in length. The back of the Northern Flicker is brown with heavy, black bars and the underside is light-buff with dark spots. The most conspicuous identifying feature is the white rump patch seen in flight as well as the bright-yellow underwings seen in flight. The cap is a light-gray and the back of the nape is red. The lower part of the neck sports a black crescent which separates the spotted breast from the unspotted throat. The male has a black stripe arising from the base of the beak going back across the cheek, commonly called a "moustache." Their call is a loud *flicka flicka flicka* or *wic wic wic wic* or sometimes a single note: *kleep*.

In Florida, the Northern Flicker is a permanent resident and breeds throughout the state, although not as commonly in the south and in the Keys. It is common in parks and open woodland areas and has adapted quite well to suburbia where it can find trees in which to nest. During the winter many migrating Northern Flickers invade Florida and the southern states and they become more widespread. The Northern Flicker can be something of a nuisance as well because some of them drum on buildings to attract a mate or to get at insects. The homeowner can usually effectively scare them away with persistence.

The Northern Flicker nests in tree cavities although many people are having success with them in nest boxes. Nesting may occur as early as March and a second brood may be produced by late spring. Generally five to eight white eggs are laid and both parents incubate for about two weeks. The young are fed regurgitated food for about four weeks at which time they are able to fledge. Successful nest cavities are used repeatedly, year after year.

Two broods are more common in the southern states than in the northern states. First broods in Florida are usually larger than the second brood. The broods in the northern states are a bit larger than where two broods are common.

Northern Flicker

Yellow-bellied Sapsucker   *Sphyrapicus varius*

The Yellow-bellied Sapsucker is a winter resident in Florida, migrating from the north and spending the winter in Florida, the Carolinas and into Tennessee and Kentucky. The breeding range of this woodpecker is declining and seems to be limited to the northern tier of eastern states and eastern Canada. Even in some of its original range it is absent. In Florida they can be found nearly everywhere there are a few trees. They arrive in Florida in late September and early October and remain until the following April; some remain into the beginning of May.

At only about eight inches tall the Yellow-bellied Sapsucker is not one of the largest of the woodpeckers. Its back is black with white or buff-colored markings. Two white wing patches are prominent both at rest and in flight. The underside is a pale yellow, hence the name "yellow-bellied," with some black streaking along the flanks. Both sexes have a black "bib" on the upper chest; the male has a red throat and the female, white. The facial patterns are similar except for the throat patch. The forecrown is red-and-black and white stripes mark the rest of the head. From the top of the head to the base of the neck it is black. A small white rump patch is evident in flight but is not as evident as in the Northern Flicker. Their call is a downward slurred *chirrrrr* or some-times a quick *pee-ek*, which it gives when alarmed in hiding.

The term "sapsucker" comes from the group of woodpeckers that make a ring-shaped hole in the cambium of the tree. These holes are evenly spaced and the concentric rows of holes are also evenly spaced. This boring is similar to tapping for maple sap to make maple sugar and syrup. The sap which flows from the holes is drunk by the woodpecker and, more importantly, it is used to lure insects which are then captured and eaten. A Yellow-bellied Sapsucker may make rings of holes on as many as a half-dozen trees, which it then visits throughout the day to gather the sweet sap and insects.

Over the years the Yellow-bellied Sapsucker has learned which trees provide the best sap to attract insects and it will return year after year to the same tree, although it will have to make new holes every year. The holes in trees can be seen for scores of years and do not normally damage the tree.

Yellow-bellied Sapsucker

Red-bellied Woodpecker *Melanerpes carolinus*

The Red-bellied Woodpecker is the most numerous and widespread of Florida's resident woodpeckers, where it is found virtually all over the entire state, except the Dry Tortugas. It is common in suburban areas as well as parklands and forests. It is adaptable to most forest types, both deciduous and tropical. It will build its nest in a variety of trees: Cypress Palms, Bald Cypresses, Live Oaks and many varieties of pine.

The Red-bellied Woodpecker is medium-to-large in size and is quite beautiful. The head is pale buff-brown with red running from the top of the bill to the shoulder. The female's red is interrupted with a gray patch. The underside is the same pale buff-brown with the red blotches at the base of the legs, hence the name "Red-bellied." The back has a black-and-white ladder effect leading to the misappellation, "Ladder-back Woodpecker."

The Red-bellied Woodpecker is primarily an eastern woodpecker but can be found throughout the southeast as well. They seem to be expanding their northern limits which process may be aided by the great increase in the popularity of birdfeeding. The extreme northern populations of Red-bellied Woodpecker migrate every winter.

A true cavity-nester, this woodpecker takes about ten days to excavate a new home. Most often they will place their nests in a dead snag, but upon occasion they can be found in a live tree with a dead center. The Cabbage Palm is a favorite in Florida for the Red-bellied Woodpecker. The nest hole can be as close to the ground as two feet or as much as one hundred feet, but most often it is between ten and fifty feet above the ground. They will take readily to birdhouses where tree cavities are at a premium.

In early April four to six white eggs are laid in the nest and are lined with tree pieces. Both sexes incubate for two weeks and the young are able to leave after about another four weeks. Young birds will follow the adults for several days after fledging. In Florida, two broods are not uncommon and occasionally three may be raised.

A bit more cosmopolitan in their eating habits, the Red-bellied Woodpecker will eat a lot of insects on trees but also will take a variety of fruit and nuts. Similar to the Red-headed Woodpecker it may hoard nuts. In fruit areas, it may even become a pest because they eat and damage oranges. Similar to the Northern Flicker, the Red-bellied Woodpecker will forage on the ground where it may take grasshoppers, ants and any other insects.

Red-bellied Woodpecker

Hairy Woodpecker and Downy Woodpecker

Picoides villosus and Picoides pubescens

The Hairy Woodpecker and Downy Woodpecker are very much alike, except for size. Of the two, the Downy Woodpecker is the more common. Both are permanent, widespread residents in Florida, although the populations of Hairy Woodpecker are declining due to the loss of trees.

The backs of both woodpeckers are black and their wings black with white spots and markings. The front is also white. The head has a black cheek patch with white markings above and below outlining the black patch. The white may reach around to the back on some birds. The males of both species have red patches on the back of the head, sometimes meeting the white. The bill of the nine-inch Hairy Woodpecker is about twice the width of the head. The six-inch Downy Woodpecker has a short bill, about half the width of the head. Both birds have black center feathers and white outer tail feathers. The Downy Woodpecker may show some black markings on the outer white tail feathers. Both birds give a whinny call and a solitary *peek*; with the Hairy Woodpecker's call being more slurred and lower-pitched.

These two birds are tree cavity nesters and are limited in range partly because of lack of suitable nest cavities. Most often they excavate their own nest cavities, but they will sometimes they will take over existing holes. One difference between them is that the female Downy Woodpecker usually selects the nest site, whereas the male Hairy Woodpecker usually selects its site. In both cases both sexes will incubate and brood the young. Incubation for both species lasts about two weeks; a day or so longer in the Hairy Woodpecker's case.

The young are fed a diet of regurgitated insects and will leave the nest in about four weeks. The young may accompany the adults for a few weeks after fledging. For the Downy Woodpecker in the northern part of the United States, one brood is most common—in Florida, two broods are possible. The Hairy Woodpecker rarely has more than one brood even in the south.

The Downy Woodpecker is the most common woodpecker to come to birdfeeders throughout the United States. In the winter it will eat suet as well as sunflower seeds. The normal diet of these woodpeckers is predominately insects but they will take seeds and berries, especially during the fall and winter. A suet/peanut butter mixture seems to be a favorite of both these woodpeckers.

Although they will use nest boxes for roosting in winter, it is rare that these birds will actually nest in a man-made box. Of the two it is more likely that the Hairy Woodpecker will use a nest box, possibly due to the lack of natural nest cavities.

Hairy Woodpecker (left) and Downy Woodpecker (right)

Eastern Kingbird *Tyrannus tyrannus*

In Florida, the Eastern Kingbird is a migratory bird as well as a summer resident. During the winter it migrates to South America. Except for in the Florida Keys, this bird is quite common and during the nesting season can be found in shrubby areas, open fields, open woodlands and park spaces. Not particularly fond of suburbia they are not usually found in our back yards except where they adjoin a field or a scrubby or natural area.

The Eastern Kingbird is fairly large at eight inches tall. It is a striking bird with a black back and white to light-gray undersides. The tail is black with a conspicuous white band across the very tip. This white band is quite evident when the bird is in flight or hovering. As in many of the kingbirds there is a characteristic red spot on the top of the head which is seldom seen unless the red crest is in an agitated state. The bill of the Eastern Kingbird has bristles at the base which are not noticeable unless you are very close.

The Eastern Kingbird sits on wires, fences or posts and flies out to capture insects, often hovering above the prey. It is also very feisty and will attack all kinds of larger birds that may threaten their young or nest including hawks, crows and Blue Jays. While hovering the Eastern Kingbird's wings beat very fast almost as if they are quivering. When hovering or flying the Kingbird makes a rapid series of nasal notes sounding like *kit kit kit kitter kitter*, picking up speed at the end.

Although migrating birds and summer residents begin arriving in March, nesting does not begin until May. The Eastern Kingbird prefers to nest in shrubs, but it has been known to build nests in tall trees. The nest is built on a horizontal branch about mid-way between the trunk and edge. Another favorite place to nest is out in the open on a post or snag. Adult birds will attack and scold you if you approach the nest too closely.

The nest is made of weeds and grasses and lined with fine grasses and feathers. The light-colored eggs are marked with brown blotches; four eggs are usually laid. Incubation is the duty of the female, and takes about two-and-a-half weeks. The young are attended by both parents and fledge in two-and-a-half weeks. Since only one brood is produced the young may remain with the parents for an extended period of time. By the end of October the summer residents and migratory kingbirds leave Florida.

The diet of this bird is predominately insects although some berries are taken. Meal worms will often entice these beautiful birds to a feeder. Occasionally they will become a nuisance as they take honey bees from beehives. This trait has given the Eastern Kingbird the nick name "Bee Martin."

Eastern Kingbird

Scissor-tailed Flycatcher *Tyrannus forficatus*

The Scissor-tailed Flycatcher is truly unforgettable. At twelve to fifteen inches long, the Scissor-tailed Flycatcher with its long scissor-like tail is not only unmistakable but beautiful as well. The Scissor-tail Flycatcher is a soft-gray color over the head, upper chest and back. The head has the typical red spot and, because of the gray, it is a little more noticeable. The wings are black but this is where the similarity ends. The flanks, underwings and undertail are a dark-peach color and are extremely colorful, especially in flight. It has been said that "you haven't seen a Scissor-tailed Flycatcher until you see the pink armpits."

The tail of the Scissor-tailed Flycatcher is longer than its body and crosses, as it name implies, in a scissor-like manner. It is divided during flight and when the wind catches it just right as it sits upon power lines and fences. The outer feathers of the tail are white and accented by the black inner feathers. Only the adults have the long tail feathers; immature birds having tails less than half the length of the adults. The outer white feathers in the tail make it appear as though the tail is extremely thin and wispy. The facial bristles common to the flycatchers are present although they are not large and noticeable.

The Scissor-tailed Flycatcher sits on a power line or fence and quietly waits for an insect to come into view, then flies from the perch and "hawks" the insect from the air. The bristles at the base of the bill are used to capture the insects, much like the Goatsucker's. Flying insects are the main diet but upon occasion some berries will be taken, typically in late summer or fall.

In Florida, the Scissor-tailed Flycatcher is a winter visitor in the extreme southern parts of the state down into the Florida Keys. When visiting Florida from south of Miami down to the Keys, watch the wires and open snags for these colorful and beautiful birds. On the Gulf Coast, and more rarely on the Atlantic Coast, they may be seen in migration as they head north to their breeding grounds or south to Mexico and Central America. Some years individual wanderers may show up anywhere in the United States as they seem to occasionally have wanderlust.

Scissor-tailed Flycatcher

Great Crested Flycatcher *Myiarchus crinitus*

About the same general size and shape as the Eastern Kingbird, the Great Crested Flycatcher is found in a completely different habitat. The tail is a bit longer giving it a slightly larger look than the Kingbird. The habitat of the Great Crested Flycatcher is woodlands, which in Florida limits the areas it will be found. It can be quite common in the proper habitat as a nesting bird and is a winter resident in the extreme southern parts of Florida.

This nine-inch bird is black on the head, back and throat. The chest and belly are lemon-yellow all the way to the base of the tail. The bill is fairly large and typically flattened as the flycatchers are, with the common bristles at the base. The lower mandible may have some yellow in it. The tail will show a pale-rust in it when in flight and some in the primary feathers of the wing. When disturbed or defending its territory the Great Crested Flycatcher will raise the feathers on its head giving it a distinct crest. The call is a loud guttural *creeep* or *weee* or repeated several times, *creep creep creep*. There are two variations of the call: one a little more guttural and the other more melodic and sweet. This melodic, sweet call is common in Florida woodlands during the summer.

A forest bird, the Great Crested Flycatcher nests in tree cavities. It does not excavate the cavity itself but will take over a woodpecker house or use a naturally-rotted cavity. The nest will be built to within a few inches of the top of the cavity. Nest material almost always includes bits of snakeskin. Not terribly fussy about nesting material it will use whatever is available, including pieces of plastic wrap as a snakeskin substitute. The Great Crested Flycatcher uses fur, feathers, leaves, string, rope, leaves and various other vegetation as available. Five cream-colored eggs marked with brown are laid in the nest in April and are incubated for about two weeks by the female. Both parents will take care of the young after hatching and they will fledge in about three weeks. One brood a year is produced.

The Great Crested Flycatcher primarily eats insects from the woodland. It has also been known to eat small lizards and salamanders if the opportunity should arise. During the fall and migration some berries may be eaten.

Nest boxes have some success in attracting the Great Crested Flycatcher when placed in the proper habitat. Occasionally when a Purple Martin house is overtaken by trees they will attempt to nest in it.

Great Crested Flycatcher

Red-eyed Vireo *Vireo olivaceus*

Although not popular or easily recognized, the Red-eyed Vireo is an abundant migratory bird as well as a summer resident in the central parts and the north. However, only on occasion will they breed in south Florida. Most often the Red-crested Vireo can be found in hardwood or mixed-hardwood forests, only occasionally in coniferous forests. In older well-established communities with large trees the Red-eyed Vireo may become a breeder.

The Red-eyed Vireo is dark-olive overall with a light-gray breast. The crown is a bluish-gray with a white eye-stripe bordered on the top and bottom with a black line. The lower black line goes through the eye. It has a red eye which is very difficult to see unless you are very close. The bill is black with a slight downcurve to it. The red eye is absent in young birds until they return in the spring.

The most common way to identify this bird is by its sweet song. If you go into any woodland during the summer, you will hear this bird calling at any time of the day and night. The call is a combination of short, usually double, phrases sung constantly. The phrases *look up*, *see me*, *up here*, *way up*, *way high* are some of the sounds the Red-eyed Vireo makes. The female sings even at the nest. This bird will sing all day, making thousands of calls.

The diet of the Red-eyed Vireo is mostly insects taken from the leaves of trees. A slower, more deliberate, feeder than the warblers, the Red-eyed Vireo will hop around the ends of branches, inspecting both sides of the leaves, stems and twigs, and take what insects, spiders or small snails it finds. In late fall during migration, the Red-eyed Vireo will take berries from the Poison Ivy, Dogwood and Myrtle.

The nest of the Red-eyed Vireo is quite elaborate. It is built in a fork of a twig, usually somewhere between ten to fifty feet above the ground. The female selects the site and builds the nest from a variety of plant fibers. It is lined with fine grass, rootlets, plant down, bark from grapevines and small leaves. The nest is fastened by spider webs and woven plant fibers. The exterior is camouflaged with lichens.

Four or five eggs are laid in the nest about the first of May and the eggs are incubated for two weeks. The eggs are white and have dark-brown spots concentrated at one end. This bird, along with the Wood Thrush, is very susceptible to Cowbird predation. Both parents take care of the young and they will leave the nest in less than two weeks. Two broods can be raised per year except in the far north where one is the rule.

Red-eyed Vireo

Northern Rough-winged Swallow

Stelgidopteryx serripennis

The Northern Rough-winged Swallow, or Sand Swallow, is a fairly common summer resident in the northern two-thirds of Florida. In the fall and spring, it is abundant as a migrant as it heads north to nest in the rest of the United States. Only in a small band that stretches across central Florida is it considered a permanent resident, present at all seasons. Some birds will winter in the state from the central part south although not in great numbers. In Florida, the population is largely restricted by the availability of suitable nest sites.

The Northern Rough-winged Swallow is a small bird of about five-and-a-half inches. It has a dirty-brown back and buff-brown throat that grades into the light-colored breast and belly. The Northern Rough-winged Swallow lacks the throat band of the Bank Swallow, although it is similarly-colored above and both can be found in the same habitats. The Northern Rough-winged Swallow has long, pointed wings, streamlined for capturing insects on the fly. Its bill is very tiny and soft, but the gape is large to capture insects. The body is streamlined for aerial maneuvering. This swallow gets its name from the rough, serrated edge of the outer primary wing feathers, the function of which is unknown.

This swallow can usually be found near waterways where it captures insects as they come off the water. In the non-breeding season, it can be found in open areas swooping over the ground in search of insects. The height that the swallows fly above the ground is supposedly a good indication of future weather: when they fly high it will be fair, but if they fly close to the ground, foul weather is not far off. During fall migration, these birds can be found in huge flocks.

The nests of the Northern Rough-winged Swallow are usually placed at the end of tunnels in banks along streams, canals or gravel pits. The nest burrows are usually four to five feet long and the nest chamber is at the end. The nest is a conglomerate of materials from grasses, both heavy and fine, to leaves. Unlike many of the other swallows, the nest almost never contains white feathers. The Northern Rough-winged Swallow will also nest in man-made cavities such as drain pipes, culverts and crevices in bridges and wharfs.

Five to six white eggs are laid in the nest and are incubated by the female for twelve to fifteen days. Both parents will feed the young for about three weeks until they fledge. Nesting occurs during May and the young are flying by about mid-summer. Migrant individuals move through Florida rather early in March along with the Tree Swallows, the earliest of the migrating swallows. Winters are usually spent south of the United States in South America.

Northern Rough-winged Swallow

Barn Swallow   *Hirundo rustica*

The Barn Swallow is probably the most recognized of all the swallows. This bird has the long, divided, "swallow tail" as well as the streamlined body, pointed wings and swooping graceful flight. These birds are dark-blue above with their undersides a buff- or deep-rust color. Young birds are not as rust-colored underneath as adults. The throat is a deep mahogany-color with a partially blue neck band extending from the back. The forehead has the same rust-color on it as the breast. In flight, the deeply-forked tail exhibits white spots which make this bird totally different from other swallows.

At about seven-inches, the Barn Swallow is not as large as the Purple Martin but is larger than the Northern Rough-winged Swallow. In flight, the Barn Swallow gives off a series of *szweet szweet* sounds.

The courtship of Barn Swallows is interesting to watch. The pair will fly in long, drawn-out flights, then land on a wire and continue the courtship. They sit next to each other and rub, twist their heads on each other, and preen each other. During courtship the pair gives a series of twitters and guttural chortles, interspersed with little pops like cracking gum.

In Florida until a few years back, the Barn Swallow was considered a transient or migrant, passing through the state to its nesting grounds or wintering areas. During the 1950s some pairs began nesting in Florida and today they have expanded their range to the Keys. However, no great numbers nest in Florida and in some cases re-nesting does not occur. In other parts of the southeast the same has happened, and nesting has increasingly spreading southward. The winter months are devoid of the Barn Swallows as they have flown south to Central and South America.

The Barn Swallow typically builds its nest in barns on a beam, ledge or shelf. They also build their nests under bridges, culverts, cliffs, caves and outdoor pavilions. The nest is constructed of mud pellets that are cemented together to form a half-cup. It usually takes the parents more than a week to build the nest. The nest is lined with coarse grass and feathers. Old nests are repaired and used again.

Four to five white eggs with brown markings are laid in the nest and incubated for about two weeks. The incubation is shared by both sexes. Young are fed regurgitated insects and are able to leave the nest in about three weeks. The last week or so the young have outgrown the nest and will sit around the top of it, from which the young can fall to be easily taken by predators. Young birds will return to the nest to roost for a short time after fledging. Parent birds will re-nest shortly, often in the same nest. The same families will return to the same successful nesting areas for years.

Barn Swallow

Purple Martin *Progne subis*

The Purple Martin is the largest of the swallows in North America. Indians were the first to attract this bird, using gourds for them to nest in and man has been making all kinds of houses ever since to attract this pretty bird. Much myth and mystique exists about this bird including that the Purple Martin is a major controller of mosquitoes, which is absolutely false. Nevertheless this bird is quite an asset to the back yard. It is very colonial and extremely bubbly in its calls, always seeming happy.

The male is a deep royal-blue, almost black, over the entire body and about eight-and-a-half-inches long. The female is dark above but has a light-gray underside. The tail is slightly forked and the bill is small, but as in all the swallows the gape is large for catching insects.

The Purple Martin nests throughout Florida. It arrives in January and February, with nesting beginning in March. The first arrivals are called "scouts" and they are usually adult males. Although the Purple Martin used to nest in tree cavities, today they predominately nest in man-made houses, some of which are quite elaborate. Some studies indicate that the old gourds that the Indians used are still the best.

Five or six white eggs are laid in the nest which is cemented together with mud and lined with grass, leaves and feathers. The female incubates the eggs for about two-and-a-half weeks. Both parents take care of the young for about four weeks until fledging. As the chicks develop their flight feathers, they may come to the front of the house and sit on the front rail if one is available. The traditional martin house with two rows of three nest chambers is not very efficient in attracting the greatest number of Purple Martins because one male will defend all three cavities and will not allow another nesting pair into the house. Houses which are hexagonal or ones with porch dividers are best. Up to three broods can be produced during one season.

In Florida the birds are ready to begin fall migration by mid-summer when huge flocks, numbering in the thousands, gather to return to South America. Most of the resident martins have left Florida by the time the northern birds invade the state. You can see the Purple Martin in Florida in virtually every month, but winter sightings are rare.

The northern populations have been declining over the last years, while the southern populations seem to be increasing. The best way to attract these birds is with the proper house in the proper location: wide open spaces, near human dwellings, and near water if possible. Houses should be kept free from competition from European Starlings and House Sparrows.

Purple Martin

Scrub Jay *Aphelocoma coerulescens*

The Scrub Jay, also called the Florida Jay, is found in central Florida and along most of the Atlantic coast, but is absent from north and south Florida. Today, because of loss of habitat, the populations in Florida are declining and the Scrub Jay is officially on the Florida threatened wildlife list. Its habitat is mixed woodlands, scrub lands, brushy forest edges and scrubby oaks. The oaks are especially important because they provide food as well as shelter and nest sites. Some of the most productive areas to see this bird are Merritt Island National Wildlife Refuge, the state parks, city parks and other wildlife preserves.

The Scrub Jay is about one-foot long and has the typical "jay-shape" although it does not carry the crest as does the common Blue Jay. The tail and wings are bright-blue as well as the head and back of the neck. The Florida birds have a light-gray forehead that is absent in the western birds. The back has a gray-brown patch in the middle. The throat is a streaked light-gray and the underside a darker-gray. A black facial patch extends from the back of the bill and covers the side of the head and is bordered by the blue cap on top and the gray throat beneath. The call of the Scrub Jay is a loud, rasping *keesh keesh* often given in flight.

The Scrub Jay has a varied diet but is particularly fond of acorns. During the breeding season, the food source is primarily insects, any invertebrate, bird's eggs and even fledgling birds. In fact, the jays have a habit of robbing nests of eggs and baby birds. After breeding and during the winter, seeds and nuts become a greater portion of the diet. These birds have been known to cache away seeds and especially acorns.

As a permanent resident, the nesting may begin as early as March or as late as May. The nest is usually placed in a small tree or some shrubs. The nest is constructed of twigs, often oak twigs and lined with finer twigs, grass, rootlets, hair and moss. The nest is quite intricate for such a large bird.

Five light-green eggs marked with fine reddish-brown spots are incubated for two-and-a-half weeks by the female. About the same amount of time is required for the young to fledge and leave the nest while attended by both parents, although the female takes most of the responsibility. Some help is available because these birds are cooperative breeders. Although they may not mate for life as in Canada Geese, pair bonds are built that last a long time. Breeding territories become feeding territories for the rest of the year, so the same birds will remain in the same area.

Scrub Jay

Blue Jay   *Cyanocitta cristata*

Probably no other bird has been loved or hated by so many. The Blue Jay is a permanent resident in Florida. Winter populations are greatly increased with migrants from the north. It is quite common where suitable habitat is available, mainly woodland or partial woodland. It has adapted quite well to modern day suburbia. The reason it creates such mixed emotions is because of its habits and beauty. At birdfeeders it is a big bully, chasing away "preferred" birds. As in the case of most jays it is also a predator on nests and nestlings.

At just under a foot in length, the Blue Jay is primarily a bluebird with other markings. Like the Stellar Jay, the Blue Jay sports a crest. The tail is marked with black lines across it and white spots at the end. The face and underside are a soft-gray accented by a black necklace. The wings also sport black bands and white spots.

Blue Jays are very noisy, calling *jay jay jay* but they have a number of other calls and sounds. The jay call is usually given in alarm or warning. Another interesting call sounds like the squeaky handle of an old-fashioned water pump. When moving through the forest or neighborhood they make a sweet *weedle weedle* call to keep in contact. The jay also imitates the call of the Red-shouldered and Red-tailed Hawks.

Blue Jays will eat most anything. They have, of course, learned to love birdseed and even have learned to eat dog and cat food from the dish. Normally the Blue Jay eats insects and small invertebrates during the summer and breeding season and seeds and berries at other times of the year. The Blue Jay has been known to steal birds eggs from nests and small nestlings. This is why small birds constantly mob the Blue Jay during the nesting season.

A nest of twigs is constructed during the spring, sometimes as early as March. The nest is fairly substantial and is generally located on a horizontal branch five to twenty feet off the ground. Mud may be used to hold the nest together but the inner lining is fine rootlets, plant material and just about anything that works and that the Blue Jay can find. Some people have successfully placed colorful yarn around the yard for the Blue Jay to use in their nests, making them easier to spot.

Four or five light-colored eggs marked with brown blotches are incubated for about eighteen days by both parents. The young will take about three weeks to leave the nest, however, they will remain together as a family for a time. Most people don't notice these birds at the nest or even as they construct it. The Blue Jay can be quite secretive and quiet. In Florida up to three broods may be produced, whereas in the North only one is common.

Blue Jay

Fish Crow *Corvus ossifragus*

The Fish Crow is smaller than the American Crow and is best identified by its call, a hoarse, almost concerned-sounding *awh oh*. The Fish Crow does not make the true *caw* of the American Crow but does make a *car* sound, somewhat similar to that of an immature American Crow. Typical of the crows it is completely black all over, even its legs are black.

The Fish Crow is primarily a coastal bird found over most of Florida but is limited to the coastal areas up the Atlantic coast almost to Cape Cod. It is also found along the Gulf Coast to the Mississippi and up river to southern Indiana, Illinois and Ohio. It also extends into the coastline of Texas. Their range on the Atlantic seems to be expanding northward. Their range in Florida is also expanding southward into the Keys. This small crow has become increasingly used to humans near the coastal towns and has adapted well to urban life, expanding its range accordingly.

Preferring coastal waters with tides and river systems, this crow eats a variety of aquatic organisms including crayfish, snails, crabs, amphibians, reptiles, insects and many other invertebrates and small vertebrates. Being a great scavenger they will also take carrion as well as raid the nests of other birds for nestlings and eggs. Florida birds have learned to drop mollusks on the rocks or pavement to crack them open to eat. They also haunt the local malls for handouts of popcorn and french fries. In some areas they can be a cause for concern to colonial nesting birds. At the proper time of the year they will take fruit, nuts and berries.

Nests are placed in the crotches of shrubs and trees from about six to fifty feet. Occasionally, they may nest nearly a hundred feet from the ground. The primary layer is of sticks and twigs, which is then built up with smaller materials. The nest is lined with leaves, hair, grass, needles and some feathers.

The eggs are a blue or green color marked heavily with brown blotches. Incubation is shared for two-and-a-half weeks. The young remain in the nest for about three weeks. Young will follow the parents for a few weeks begging noisily for food. Only one brood is produced a year, however, if a nest is lost before hatching, another brood may be attempted. The Fish Crows will nest in small groups and are much more sociable than the American Crow. In the fall and winter huge flocks may congregate to roost.

Fish Crow

Tufted Titmouse *Parus bicolor*

In Florida this little gray bird is common except from about Sarasota south. It prefers woodlots and forests, but it can be found in scrub land and open woodland where nesting is available. State parks and refuges are good places to find the Tufted Titmouse as well as many backyard feeding stations.

The Tufted Titmouse is a relative of the Chickadees and sports a "tuft," or crest, as its name indicates. At only six inches, this little bird looks like a house mouse with its overall gray color and bright black eye. Its underside is light-colored with rust or brown on the flanks. Its feet and legs are gray, its bill short and black.

This bird gives a clear, loud whistle, *peter peter peter* or *weeder weeder weeder*. Variations are a sweet, loud *trick or treat*. When moving through the forest together they will give a little *tseet* similar to that of the Chickadee. If disturbed they will give a scolding, raspy *wheea wheea wheea*.

The Tufted Titmouse is easily to attract to feeding stations. It prefers the gray-striped sunflower, but any sunflower will be taken. Since the Tufted Titmouse doesn't have the capacity to crack open the sunflower, as do the Cardinal and Grosbeak, they take the seed away to a perch and split it open by placing it between their toes and striking it with their beak. Many people put out sunflower chips and hearts they don't have to work so hard and to lessen the mess left by hulls. During the winter the Tufted Titmouse will also eat suet, especially a mixture of suet and peanut butter. The Tufted Titmouse can even be taught to eat from your hand.

A cavity nester, the Tufted Titmouse must use a natural cavity or a cavity from a woodpecker. It will readily nest in man-made nest boxes. Nests have been found in holes as low as a couple of feet from the ground and as high as a hundred feet. The nest cavity is lined with moss, bark, leaves, fur and hair. The fur and hair seem to be important to the Titmouse as it has been seen taking it from living creatures! Like the Great Crested Flycatcher it almost always puts snakeskins in its nest. Successful nest sites are used year after year.

Five to seven white eggs with small brown markings are incubated by the female for two weeks. Young are attended by both parents for about two-and-a-half weeks to fledging. In Florida, two broods are sometimes produced; the first often in attendance on the young of the second. Parents seem to pair for life as do Chickadees.

During the winter these birds will be found in mixed flocks of Chickadees, Nuthatches and Downy Woodpeckers. Occasionally warblers or kinglets will join the group. They will set up a winter feeding territory and remain together as a group until the next breeding season.

Tufted Titmouse

Carolina Chickadee *Parus carolinensis*

The Carolina Chickadee is basically the southern counterpart to the Black-capped Chickadee and they are almost identical. There are a few minor differences. The most obvious is the call of the Carolina Chickadee is a loud, four-note *fee-bee fee-bay*. The Black-capped Chickadee has only two notes, *fee-bee*. In the smaller Carolina Chickadee, the *chickadee dee dee dee dee* call is faster and a bit higher in pitch. It would be difficult to distinguish them apart by their Chickadee call alone.

Looking closely at the coloration of the two birds, another minor difference is the line at the bottom of the black bib. The Carolina Chickadee has a rather smooth line at the bottom edge, whereas the Black-capped Chickadee has a jagged line. Also, the Carolina Chickadee has no white in the wing which can be present in the Black-capped Chickadee. Both birds have a black cap and black bib with a white cheeks. The back is a brownish-gray and the undersides are a light-gray. The Carolina Chickadee is less than five inches long.

Probably the easiest way to tell these two birds apart in Florida is that the Carolina Chickadee is the only one found here. It is quite common in the north but is not found in the southern third of Florida. It prefers deciduous woodlands, open woodlands and parklands but will frequent swamps and thickets if nest sites are available. Older suburban neighborhoods are attractive to this little bird as the trees become more mature and people provide feeding stations. From Florida north it is quite common.

Carolina Chickadee

Blue-Gray Gnatcatcher *Polioptila caerulea*

Florida is the wintering ground for a fair number of Blue-gray Gnatcatchers that nest in the north but there is also a growing resident population throughout the state. The Blue-gray Gnatcatcher is found as far north as Maine and west almost to California. It winters in the southern coastal states and Florida down to Central and South America. This chipper little bird is not as prevalent in the interior of the state and populations there may be spotty.

At about four-and-a-half inches long, this little bird appears to be mostly tail. The male is a blue-gray above with light-gray underparts. The tail is long and has white outer tail feathers. The female is a lighter gray on the back and lacks the dark eye-stripe of the male. Both sexes have white eye-rings. When you see these birds they are most often flitting about capturing food or collecting nest material. Their long tail seems to be in constant movement.

The call is a somewhat buzzy-sounding *zzee* which is repeated often and constantly. It will even call when returning to the nest so nest discovery is fairly simple.

The nest of the Blue-gray Gnatcatcher is extremely intricate. It is quite small, usually little more than an inch across. It is normally placed on a horizontal branch or fork of a branch from five to twenty-five feet above the ground. It resembles a hummingbird nest, compact and made from plant down and spider silk. The outside is covered with lichens to camouflage it so that it resembles just another knot on the branch. The inside is lined with fine plant material and more down.

The female lays four or five pale-blue eggs with small brown markings. Both parents incubate the eggs which hatch in about twelve days. In two weeks the young will leave and in Florida a second brood may be produced. In the north only one brood is produced. With the fragmentation of forests, the Blue-gray Gnatcatcher has become increasingly threatened by Cowbird predation.

The habitat of the Blue-gray Gnatcatcher is quite varied but they must have trees. They prefer woodlands near water, but will use any woodlot. City and state parks are good spots to sight these little birds. Their diet is predominately insects and other small invertebrates. Their bill is quite long and pointed and is adapted to taking small insects.

Blue-Gray Gnatcatcher

White-breasted Nuthatch and Brown-headed Nuthatch
Sitta carolinensis and Sitta pusilla

The White-breasted Nuthatch is quite common in the northern parts of the United States as it once was in Florida, where today it is in serious decline. The Brown-headed Nuthatch is often associated with the Red-cockaded Woodpecker. Both birds use the same pine trees for nesting and feeding. The White-breasted Nuthatch's habitat is almost any mature deciduous, pine or mixed forest. Perhaps the lack of mature trees is one reason for the decline of the White-breasted Nuthatch in Florida.

The White-breasted Nuthatch is also called the "Upside-down Bird" because it searches for food while hanging head down from the branch. It has a white face and underparts with a black cap and a light slate-gray back. The female has a gray forehead with black cap extending to the neck. Its bill is long and pointed, the better to remove insects from crevices and split open seeds. The Brown-headed Nuthatch is smaller at four-and-a-half inches as compared to the six-inch White-breasted Nuthatch. As its name indicates, the Brown-headed Nuthatch has a brown cap that reaches down to the eye, making the white cheek actually only half a cheek of white. At the back of the neck just above the shoulders is a white or buff-colored spot. The tail of the Brown-breasted Nuthatch is somewhat shorter than the White-breasted Nuthatch in comparison to its body.

Both Nuthatches are cavity nesters and may use nest cavities already excavated by woodpeckers or natural ones found in snags. Both Nuthatches lay from five to seven white eggs with brown markings. The females incubate the eggs for about two weeks until hatching. Brooding and caring for the young is shared and it is another two weeks until the young leave the nest. The fledging of the Brown-headed Nuthatch takes a few days longer than the White-breasted Nuthatch.

The Nuthatches are much like woodpeckers in that they forage for insects in the bark and crevices of trees. They don't have the chiseling capabilities of woodpeckers, but they can pry and probe in the bark. The Nuthatches spiral downward on the trunk of a tree to get into places that woodpeckers may not see on their way up. Brown-headed Nuthatches have been observed using pieces of bark to pry up other pieces of bark to expose insects and insect eggs. Young birds are fed a diet high in protein, mainly insects. After nesting season, seeds and berries may be taken as well as sunflower seeds from our feeders. The Nuthatches do not have the ability to crush the seeds and cannot hold the seeds in their toes, as can Chickadees or Tufted Titmice, so they must shove the seed into a crevice and chisel it open.

White-breasted Nuthatch (top)
Brown-headed Nuthatch (bottom)

Brown Thrasher *Toxostoma rufum*

The Brown Thrasher isn't really a thrush at all. In fact, it is more closely related to the Mockingbird. It is called a "mini-thrush" because it mimics the calls of other birds and animals. The other mimic is the Northern Mockingbird. The Brown Thrasher resembles the thrushes that spend the winter in Florida.

The way to distinguish the calls of the Brown Thrasher from the real thing is that their calls are repeated almost always in pairs, that is to say the phrases are repeated before going on to the next phrase. The imitations are very good. I have heard perfect imitations of Sora Rails and Kingbirds. Often you can tell which birds the Thrasher spent the winter with as that is the phrase most often mimicked. The Brown Thrasher may have well over 1,000 calls, the largest number of any songbird in North America. It is even said that one Thrasher imitated the school bell so well that school was actually dismissed early several times.

This foot-long bird is rather striking with its rust-red upper parts, long, rust-colored tail and heavily streaked breast. The base color of the breast is tan with dark-brown streaking. The wingbars are also buff and the bill is long and slightly downcurved, typical of many thrashers. The tail is nearly as long as the rest of the body. The sexes are similar in plumage.

Their eyes are yellow and are a great accent to the rust-colored body.

The Brown Thrasher is a common bird of scrubby areas, forest edges, shrub land, open woodlands and parks. It has adapted well to backyards that have a good variety of well-established shrubs. The Brown Thrasher is also found in cemeteries.

Nests are usually built in April and May in shrubs fairly close to the ground, normally not more than five or six feet tall. In some parts of the United States they build the nest right on the ground. The nest is fairly massive at nearly a foot across and is made of twigs, roots and vines mixed with leaves. The inner nest is lined with finer roots, vines and grasses.

Five pale-blue eggs spotted with rust are incubated by both parents for two weeks. After a heavy diet of protein-rich insects the young will fledge in two weeks. The parents will be tenacious in defense of the nest, challenging anything that comes near, a trait also of the Mockingbird. When disturbed the Brown Thrasher gives a call that is sort of a bark, possibly to warn the young or to unnerve the intruder.

The diet of the Brown Thrasher is mainly insects during the summer but includes berries and seeds when fall and winter arrive. In Florida, the winter population is greatly augmented by migrating birds from the north.

Brown Thrasher

Northern Mockingbird   *Mimus polyglottos*

The Northern Mockingbird is Florida's state bird and is the bird most often recognized by southern residents. This bird belongs to the group of birds called the "mimic thrushes" because they reproduce the sounds of other birds and a variety of other creatures quite accurately. The mimic calls can be so accurate it is almost impossible to separate them from the real thing. The Mockingbird usually gives the call in groups of three or more; the Catbird does not repeat them but keeps adding new calls; and the Brown Thrasher makes the call twice.

The Northern Mockingbird is a ten-inch long, slender bird with a long tail. It is predominately gray on the upper parts of the body with white underneath. The tail is bordered by white feathers and there are large splashes of white in the wings while in flight. The wings have two wing bars and some of the white spots are visible when they are folded.

Today the Mockingbird is a common resident of suburbia as well as most any park or wayside area. The Mockingbird has adapted well to agricultural areas and can be found in most edge or transitional habitats. It prefers to nest in shrubs about five to eight feet above the ground, rarely exceeding ten feet. The nest is rather bulky with a base of twigs, built mainly by the male and then lined with rootlets, fine leaves, grass and other soft plant material by the female. The nest is similar to the Brown Thrasher.

The three to five light greenish-blue eggs are speckled with blotches of brown. The eggs are incubated for twelve to thirteen days before hatching. Two weeks later the young will fledge. Both parents attend the young.

During courtship the male and female will do a mating dance on the ground with their heads and tails erect and wings spread. The run toward each other and then retreat. They repeat the run and even fly into the air. Unsuccessful males will continue to sing to attract a female even into the late hours of the night. In Florida nesting begins in March and continues into late summer with up to four broods.

This abundant and common bird of Florida is fond of almost any fruit or insect. Mockingbirds have a unique way of capturing insects, called "hawking." They give a "wing flash," a sudden, quick rise to the wings to flash the white in them, when walking on the ground. Then they slowly lower the wing to watch for any insect startled by this movement.

The Northern Mockingbird can be enticed to feeders which have fruit, cooked vegetables, suet or insects. Of course, in the case of all birds, water is essential. During the winter the population of the Mockingbird swells with northern migrants.

Northern Mockingbird

Gray Catbird *Dumetella carolinensis*

The Gray Catbird is a nesting bird of the northern half of Florida and is most abundant when invasions of northern migrants spend the winter. This bird is one of the trio of birds called the "mimic thrushes." It is also the smallest, at nine inches. This slim bird can be found in brushy shrub land, woodland edges, park edges, stream edges, more mature suburban landscaping and poorly-manicured parks.

The Gray Catbird bird is a dark-gray overall with some subtle markings which are interesting to note. The least obvious of these is the undertail coverts. The base of the undertail sports a rich orange-rust patch not readily noticeable. The top of the head or cap is black.

Like the Northern Mockingbird and Brown Thrasher, the Catbird will mimic the calls of other birds and animals. Unlike the Mockingbird and Brown Thrasher, the Catbird doesn't repeat the calls but gives a long series of different calls before pausing.

The Gray Catbird gets its name because of its color and the fact that it makes a perfect mewing call, imitating a lost cat or kitten. This cat-like mew will often be interspersed with other calls. It will also give the mew when upset as well as a *clucking* or *check* sounds. These two calls, when given repeatedly, are cause for other birds to come and investigate and scold the Gray Catbird. The Carolina Wren also gives an alarm call that triggers the same response in birds.

It is surprising how similar the three mimics are in their nest building. Like the Mockingbird, the male Gray Catbird begins to build the basic foundation of the nest while the female does the final building and lining. The nest is fairly bulky and is built in shrubs, tangles, briars or small trees. The Gray Catbird prefers that the nest be invisible and will select a very dense vegetative site. The male builds the base out of sticks, vines, large leaves, weeds and grasses. The female lines the nest with finer materials: fine grasses and small roots.

The eggs are bluish-green in color. Often the nest is confused with the American Robin but the Gray Catbird uses no mud and the Robin prefers more open sites. The female alone incubates the eggs for about two weeks but both parents will take care of the young until they fledge, about two weeks later. The young are fed a variety of insects but may also be given berries in season. In Florida, two broods are common.

Not normally a seed eater the Gray Catbird can be attracted to a feeding station with suet or a mixture of suet and peanut butter. The most successful way to attract these birds is by putting out a shallow bird bath with moving water. During the Florida summer, the number of birds attracted to the bath is remarkable.

Gray Catbird

Cedar Waxwing *Bombycilla cedrorum*

The Cedar Waxwing does not nest in Florida but can be found here most of the year. It is most abundant during the winter migration from October until late April. Called "vagabond migrants," Cedar Waxwings spend the winter in huge flocks wherever berries and insects can be found. When the food is gone they leave. A favorite place to see these beautiful birds is along ponds, rivers and other waterways where they sit on a branch along the shore, flitting out to capture insects arising from or descending to the water.

The Cedar Waxwing, at seven inches, is exquisite in its coloration. The body is a rich light-brown with the underbelly grading to a pale-yellow. The wings are a gray-brown and some secondary feathers on the wings are tipped with a red, wax-like color, hence the name "Waxwing." The tail has a bright-yellow band across the end. The head is crested with a black facial mask bordered partially by white stripes.

The call of the Cedar Waxwing is a high pitched twitter or *zeee* given in flight and when foraging. When a flock takes off in flight they will all begin calling as if to say "OK, guys lets go!"

The Cedar Waxwing is a very communal bird. During the non-breeding season it will create huge feeding flocks which can number into the hundreds. In these flocks the Cedar Waxwing is quite tame and can be approached very closely. Even during the nesting season they will remain in small colonies, sometimes even nesting in the same tree or group of trees. When feeding in these nest groups, they will leave together and return together. When fledged the young then become a part of this group, which may then combine with a couple of other smaller nesting colonies.

The diet of the Cedar Waxwing is primarily berries and insects. The bill of the Cedar Waxwing is relatively small but the gape is fairly large. Initially the young are fed insects, but berries are added to their diet as they become older. After the ice thaws the crab apples and cranberries ferment, and the Cedar Waxwing, when devouring them, can become quite a lush. It is not uncommon to see them lying about the tree in various stages of inebriation!

The mating dance, or "side hop," is elaborate. One bird picks up a berry and sidles up to the prospective mate. It then hops a couple of hops away, then hops back again, passing the berry to the other bird. The prospective mate then hops sideways a couple of hops and then hops back and hands the berry back. This "side hopping" can be repeated for weeks. There is nothing funnier than to see a tree full of Cedar Waxwings, all engaged in doing the "side hop."

Cedar Waxwing

Carolina Wren *Thryothorus ludovicianus*

The Carolina Wren is a woodland bird and breeds throughout Florida. In Florida it is probably the most common bird of the woods. The Carolina Wren prefers mature, open woodlands with abundant understory plants but it has learned to adapt to suburbia, especially near older homes that have well-established trees and shrubs. It will nest in woodlots adjoining agricultural areas.

This wren, at five-and-a-half inches, is the largest of the wrens in the United States. It is a dark reddish-brown above with buff-cream color on the chest and belly. Wingbars are a faint row of white dots. The tail is usually held erect and has faint bars across the feathers. The head has a pronounced white eye-stripe bordered by black stripes above and below. The bill is long, pointed and slightly downcurved. The throat is white.

For such a small bird it is quite loud, possibly so that it can be heard in the deep forest. The most common call is a loud *teakettle teakettle teakettle* repeated over and over again. Occasionally, a two-note call will be given, *churry churry churry*. When disturbed or scolding the Carolina Wren will give a *pishhhing* call, which is a magnet for other little birds. When other birds hear the *pishhhhing* they will come to investigate and chime in. Birders imitate this call, which causes birds to show themselves, and as more birds come and scold, a snowballing effect occurs, attracting even more birds. The *pishhhhing* call or playing bird tapes are not to be overused or used in the breeding season because they stress the birds. Many parks, refuges and natural areas have outlawed the use of tapes and before using them you should check the regulations.

The nest of the Carolina Wren is placed in a variety of places. Traditionally they prefer cavities but they will use any nook or cranny to place a nest. One of their favorites in a suburban yard is a hanging basket or flower pot. In the wild they will use stumps, woodpecker holes, upturned tree roots and spaces between rocks. The nest is constructed of twigs, leaves, roots and bark strips. When possible the nest is domed so that the entrance is from the side. The lining is finer material such as grass, hair, moss, fur and feathers. Both parents construct the nest but the female is attended by the male when she alone incubates for about two weeks.

The eggs are cream-colored with brown markings. Both parents attend the young until fledging two weeks later. Often young birds will remain with the male as the female begins to build another nest. In Florida, two broods are common and a third brood is possible on occasion.

Carolina Wren

Eastern Bluebird   *Sialia sialis*

The Eastern Bluebird is probably one of our more successful population increase stories. In the '70s and '80s, this bird was in drastic decline and special efforts were initiated to bring them back. Florida was no exception and today this beautiful bird is making a dramatic comeback.

The Eastern Bluebird can be found throughout Florida but has been limited in the past to pine forests where it had suitable nest cavities. This has changed with the number of bluebird houses put up by individuals and groups. In winter, a large number of winter visitors come from the north which increases the population.

Primarily an insect eater, the Eastern Bluebird sits on a post, small tree or wire in a fairly open area to watch forthem. Upon seeing one it flies down and captures it and flies back to the perch to swallow it. In winter, fruit and berries become a greater portion of its diet.

The Eastern Bluebird is sky-blue over the back and upper head. Its chest, sides, side of the neck and upper belly are a dark-orange. The belly and undertail are white. The closely-related Western Bluebird has a entirely blue head and throat. About sparrow-sized, at seven inches, it appears a bit chunky. The female is not as blue above nor as rusty below.

The call is a quiet *cheer up cheerful Charlie* given from a perch or in flight. When disturbed or just inquisitive, they will give a *pik* note. Although you may hear the calls from a fairly good distance they are not loud.

One reason for the decline of the Eastern Bluebird was the lack of nest cavities; another was the usurpation of the remaining cavities by starlings and House Sparrows. Today both problems have been licked by placing numerous houses that have an entrance hole no larger than an inch-and-a-half to keep out starlings. House Sparrows can be eliminated with different traps. The interstate highway roadsides are the perfect habitat for the Eastern Bluebird—open, grassy areas with places to perch while hunting. Entire stretches of highway have been adorned with bluebird houses.

The nest cavity is usually lined with grasses, pine needles and softer plant materials. Usually five pale-blue or white eggs are incubated for two weeks by the female. The young are attended by both parents and can fledge in as little as two weeks. Young are susceptible to botfly larva and predation from House Wrens and English Sparrows. Young and juvenile birds are spotted, with brown backs with a hint of blue. Families will remain together throughout the winter. Young of the year before will help with successive nestings. Adults can sometimes successfully defend the nest, but if one parent is gone it is almost impossible. In Florida up to three broods can be produced.

Eastern Bluebird

American Robin *Turdus migratorius*

Called "Robin Redbreast" by school children, this bird is one of the most numerous winter visitors in Florida. In the last half century, it has become a fairly substantial breeder in suburban areas in the northern Florida. The American Robin can be found wherever there are berries.

At ten inches, the American Robin is our largest thrush. The back of the American Robin is brownish-black with the head and tail being gray-black. The throat is white with fine black streaking. The eye has a broken white ring around it. The chest and part of the belly are a brick-red with the lower belly being white. The bill is yellow. In flight, the tail will flash white at the outer tips. The American Robin typically hops about the lawn with its head cocked to one side looking for worms, a favorite spring and summer food. Many people think when they see the Robin's head cocked to one side, it is listening intently for worms. Actually it is looking down a worm hole for a bit of shiny worm to strike and grab.

Female American Robins are not as brightly colored, but sometimes during nesting it may be difficult to tell them apart. The Robin's call is a familiar spring song and it has a number of phrases such as *cheer up, cheerie lee, cheerie ly*—all given in succession with a definite pause between them. The Robins are the first to sing in the morning and last to sing at night. A pre-dawn chorus of Robins is a sure sign of spring. When disturbed or angry the American Robin will give a *tut tut tut* or a loud *peak peak peak*.

March is the earliest that the American Robin nests in Florida. The nesting continues until early summer, producing two to three broods. Nests are made of twigs, grasses, weeds, string and bark. The nest is lined with mud to conform to the body of the female and then lined with finer grasses. The nests are placed on a substantial limb or at the joint of a limb, on the ledge of a building with some protection, on porch columns and porch lights. Many people provide robin shelves for them to nest upon, which are also good for Eastern Phoebes and Barn Swallows.

Four or five blue eggs are incubated for about two weeks by the female. The young grow quickly on a diet of high-protein insects and can leave the nest in about sixteen days. The young will follow the parents around for a few days.

The Robin was one of the indicating birds used to illustrate the dramatic effects of using unrestricted widespread pesticides. In certain parts of the country, the robin is a pest in fruit orchards and vegetable crops. It is also a state bird for three states: Michigan, Wisconsin and Connecticut.

American Robin

Hermit Thrush   *Catharus guttatus*

Most of the thrushes are just transients in Florida, except the American Robin, Bluebird, Hermit Thrush and Wood Thrush. The Hermit Thrush is a transient and a winter resident. The thrushes have fairly big eyes and slender bills used to catch insects. They are generally characterized by having brown-shaded backs and spotted breasts. Of course, the Eastern Bluebird and American Robin lack some of these characteristics, however, the immature of these two species do have the spotted breast. All four thrushes are normally woodland birds with very fine songs.

The Hermit Thrush arrives in Florida during October and remains until the following May when it returns to the northern United States and Canada. Those birds that migrate through Florida go on to South and Central America. In Florida the Hermit Thrush can be widespread in wooded areas where it can find the proper diet. Most often it prefers moist woodlands where insects are abundant. The main diet of the Hermit Thrush is insects that it catches on the forest floor and in wooded thickets. In Florida, as well as in the north where it may remain for a portion of the winter, berries become a good food for the Hermit Thrush including: Poison Ivy, Myrtle, Dogwood, Holly, Virginia Creeper and those of various ornamentals.

The Hermit Thrush is a small thrush at just under seven inches. It has a gray-brown back with a light breast. The upper part of the breast is buff-colored with gray-brown streaks. The throat is light-colored and streak-free. The eye has a complete buff-colored eye-ring which accents the large black eye. Probably the most dominant feature is the tail, being a real rusty-red. The flanks of the bird may show a little color. In the woods it sits on a low branch and cocks its tail upwards, then lowers it slowly. It will fly down from the perch to grab an insect, much like the Eastern Bluebird.

It is possible to confuse the many thrushes that frequent Florida. However, the Hermit Thrush has a rust-colored tail. As the saying goes, "He is a hermit that sits on his red tail all day." The Wood Thrush has a rust-red head and resembles the Red-headed Woodpecker. The Gray-cheeked Thrush has a gray cheek with incomplete eye-ring. The body of the Veery is rust-red overall: he is "veery red." The Swainson's Thrush has a buff-colored breast and pronounced buff-colored eye-ring like the "boat swainsman who wears the yellow shirt and bandana."

Hermit Thrush

Wood Thrush   *Hylocichla mustelina*

The Wood Thrush is a nesting thrush of Florida along with the American Robin and the Eastern Bluebird. Its range for nesting is limited to the extreme northern parts of Florida. At no time is the Wood Thrush abundant, either in nesting or migration. The wintering birds spend their time in Central America.

The Wood Thrush is about an inch larger than the Hermit Thrush, measuring about seven-and-three-quarters of an inch. The streaking, or spots, on the Wood Thrush are extremely bold on the chest, flanks and stomach. The spots go up to, and include, the throat and the side of the head. The body color is a brown-red overall, with the head being exceptionally red. A prominent white eye-ring is present. The tail and rump are darker, almost olive.

Migrating birds, as well as nesting birds, begin arriving in Florida in March and leave by early May. Fall migration begins in October and usually is over during the same month. The Wood Thrush nests in April through May. Nesting occurs in deciduous forests or mixed forests. The nest is placed in a fork of a limb or on a horizontal branch from six to over fifty feet up in the tree. Occasionally the nest will be placed just above a game path, so that the adult can fly down to capture insects disturbed by passing game. The nest is quite bulky with the base being built of weeds, grasses, leaves, moss and bark. The cup-shaped nest is lined with mud similar to that of the American Robin. The inner nest is lined with fine grasses and rootlets. The nest base often has white paper mixed in with it, which some feel is to break up the shape against the sky. The female does all the building of the nest.

Four light-green-blue eggs are laid in the nest and incubated by the female for two weeks before hatching. The young are fed a diet of insects by both parents and will leave the nest in about twelve days. Young are dependent upon parents for some time after fledging, taking food from the parents for as long as two to three weeks. Two broods may be the norm in the southern part of the range.

As in all the thrushes, the song is quite beautiful. Being the most common woodland thrush, the Wood Thrush's song is the most recognized. The notes are flute-like with two or three phrases. Common phrases are *ee-o-lay ee-o-lee*, sometimes with a little added chortle at the end. Like the American Robin it is one of the last to sing at night and one of the first to sing in the morning.

The Wood Thrush is being seriously hurt by Cowbird predation. Fragmentation of forests has allowed the Cowbird access to the nests of these wonderful songbirds. Serious declines have been experienced over the last decade or so.

Wood Thrush

Loggerhead Shrike   *Lanius ludovicianus*

The "Butcher Bird" is another name for the Loggerhead Shrike, a permanent resident of Florida. It is a common bird except for in the extreme south and the Keys, where it is a sporadic winter visitor. Populations from the north during the winter greatly increase the numbers of Loggerhead Shrike. In areas of concentrated development, the population is declining, possibly due to the loss of habitat and food sources. The habitat of the Loggerhead Shrike is open country with scattered trees and shrubs, scrub lands, open forest and natural park lands.

The Loggerhead Shrike is a stockier bird than the Northern Mockingbird, with which it is often confused. The Loggerhead Shrike is about nine inches long and primarily gray in color. The wings and tail are black with the undersides an off-white. Small, white wing spots are visible in flight and slightly so while at rest. The outer tail feathers are also white. The most striking feature of the Loggerhead Shrike is its head. It has a black mask above the bill, unlike the Northern Shrike and it has a dark, hooked bill that it uses to catch prey. When it flies, the white in its wings is not as large or noticeable as the white in the Mockingbird wings. Although the Loggerhead Shrike is a ferocious predator, it doesn't have the grasping ability of owls and hawks.

The Loggerhead Shrike feeds on grasshoppers and crickets. It will also take mice and small lizards and, if the opportunity arises, small birds and nestlings. One unique feature of both types of shrikes is that they "store" food by impaling it on a thorn bush or barbed wire fence. This cache of food is used when young are being fed or the female is on nest.

The Loggerhead Shrike begins nesting in March with even successive broods fledged by the end of June. The nest is placed in a shrub or sometimes a small, thick tree. Usually it is placed from five to fifteen feet above the ground. The nest is well constructed of twigs, bark, weed stems and sticks. In certain parts of Florida, Spanish moss is used both for the body and the inner lining which may be grasses, plant down, feathers and rootlets. The male brings the materials but the female does the bulk of the construction.

The female also incubates the eggs as the male brings her tender morsels. Incubation of the five gray eggs marked with black or dark-gray lasts about sixteen or seventeen days. Male and female both take care of the young until they fledge at three weeks, but it may be several weeks before the young are totally left on their own and can take care of themselves. Up to three broods can be raised in Florida and the south.

Loggerhead Shrike

Eastern Meadowlark *Sturnella magna*

The Eastern Meadowlark is a resident of Florida and is common where natural grasslands or fallow fields are located. This bird can be found in agricultural fields if the crops aren't harvested before nesting is complete. The Eastern Meadowlark can be found in many of the state parks and natural areas as well.

The Eastern Meadowlark is a fairly large, stocky bird at over nine inches. The breast is a bright-yellow and is set off by a broad, black "V" on the upper breast. The sides of the bird are white with black streaks. The back is brown with buff-colored feather edges giving the back a scalloped look. The head is somewhat flattened with a long, pointed bill that is used to capture insects. The top of the head has tan and brown stripes going from the bill to the back of the head. A little yellow shows in the eye-stripe forward of the eye. In flight the white outer tail feathers are extremely noticeable. When walking on the ground it flicks its tail, constantly showing the white feathers. This may be a mechanism to frighten insects or to confuse would-be predators.

In Florida, nesting may begin in February. The courtship of the Eastern Meadowlark is quite interesting. The male picks a dancing spot and stands erect with its bill pointed skyward. It then dances around with its tail fanned out and flicking. He flaps his wings and puffs out the bright-yellow breast feathers. The male may get so excited it will jump up into the air and begin the procedure all over again. Upon acceptance the female will join the male but remains under control and stays on the ground.

The nest is built by the female, who may make a number of dummy nests before completing the final one. The nest is made entirely of heavy and light grasses and is built with a dome so entrance must come from the side. The nest is constructed to take advantage of the surrounding vegetation. Occasionally fur and hair are used to line the inner nest.

The female lays four or five eggs that are white with brown or purple markings. She alone will incubate the eggs for about two weeks. The male will help with the young, who will fledge in about twelve days. While a second nest is being built the female will still be taking care of the young from the first nest. Two broods are normal in Florida.

Winter brings an influx of birds from the north into Florida. Being predominately insect eaters, the Eastern Meadowlark finds it hard going to remain in snow-covered areas. The Eastern Meadowlark eats all sorts of insects and other invertebrates. During the summer, grasshoppers, crickets, beetles and a variety of larva are the main menu. As fall and winter approach, a few seeds make up for the declining number of insects.

Eastern Meadowlark

Yellow Warbler   *Dendroica petechia*

Suburbia has usurped the wetlands and wild areas that used to cover the eastern part of North America. Because of this some of our wetland birds have had to adjust to life in our shrubby backyards and neighborhoods. The Yellow Warbler is one of these welcome additions to our backyard habitats.

The Yellow Warbler is a yellow bird with a gray-olive back. The male has rust or brown streaks running down its breast. Some have said that these streaks appear to be tobacco juice drips. The male sings loudly from trees and shrubs most of the day. His song is three or four notes followed by three quick notes. A common mnemonic is *sweet sweet sweet I'm so sweet*. The song is musical, loud and easily remembered.

This tame little bird can be found over much of the eastern United States. In Florida, the Yellow Warbler is primarily a bird of the spring and fall when it migrates through the state. It winters from Mexico to South America.

The nests of the Yellow Warbler are placed in thick shrubs at about eye level. It is very defensive and steadfast in protecting its nest, resisting flight until absolutely necessary which makes it easy to study and admire. If you don't approach too closely it will go about its business of rearing its young and you can see the entire process from incubation to fledging.

Usually four or five off-white eggs with variable brown spots are laid and hatch in about twelve days. The nests are easy to find and are often parasitized by the Brown-headed Cowbird. If the warbler finds the eggs of the Brown-headed Cowbird, it will build another nest over them, covering them to prevent them from hatching, which gives a "layered look" to the nest. Even so the Cowbird is still successful enough to cause problems for this little warbler. If hatched, the Cowbird young drive out the other babies and take all the food and energy the parent birds can provide.

An insect eater, the Yellow Warbler gleans insects from vegetation, trees and shrubs. Occasionally a few berries will be taken.

Yellow Warbler

Yellow-rumped Warbler   *Dendroica coronata*

Formerly called the "Myrtle Warbler," the Yellow-rumped Warbler is a common winter resident in Florida as well a migratory bird as it travels to and from the breeding areas. The Yellow-rumped Warbler breeds in the extreme northern part of the United States and Canada. The western species was called "Audubon's Warbler." They were previously thought to be two different species, but now have been combined. The main physical difference is in the throat: the Audubon's Warbler has a yellow throat whereas the Myrtle Warbler has a white throat.

The Yellow-rumped Warbler is rather drab while in Florida, not being in breeding plumage. It is a small bird about five-and-a- half inches tall, gray-brown above with a streaked light underside. A white eye-line is visible in all plumages. The bright-yellow rump is the most identifying characteristics of this bird. It is present in all seasons and in both sexes. In flight, the yellow rump is quite prominent and noticeable from a great distance. Another identifying characteristic is the very distinctive call: a *chip*. This call is given when traveling in feeding flocks as well as during migration. It doesn't seem possible that a simple *chip* should be so distinctive, but once you have heard it several times you will understand.

The Yellow-rumped Warbler is the last warbler to migrate from the north, and it is commonly found during the winter as far north as Michigan or New York. In the winter, its eating habits change from insects to berries thus allowing it to survive in snow-covered areas. The Myrtle Warbler got its name because it eats the berries of the wax myrtle in the south, and in the north it eats the white berries of the poison ivy plant. It does the same in Florida where berries are eaten along with insects for the winter.

The Yellow-rumped Warbler begins to arrive in Florida from the north in October and will congregate in large flocks for the winter. They will remain in Florida and a number of the southern states for the winter. The Yellow-rumped Warbler is a common winter resident in all of the southern coastal states. Spring migration begins in late February and most all the birds have left Florida by the end of April.

Yellow-rumped Warbler

Yellow-throated Warbler   *Dendroica dominica*

The Yellow-throated Warbler is a very pretty and loud warbler. It is a fairly common permanent resident of the northern half of Florida. In the southern half of Florida it is a fairly common winter resident. In Florida, this bird can be found in mixed forests of pine and deciduous trees. In the north, it is fond of wet forests with sycamore trees, and is therefore sometimes called the "Sycamore Warbler." Spanish moss-covered trees are also preferred, especially in breeding season. In the northern part of its range (Indiana and Michigan) the populations were declining, but in recent years the populations have rebounded somewhat in forested stream sides with an abundance of mature sycamore trees.

The Yellow-throated Warbler is an insect eater. It gleans insects from the high up in the foliage of trees. Like the Nuthatches and Brown Creeper, it probes under bark and in fissures in the tree trunk for insects. It can be seen deliberately inspecting all sides of branches and twigs, and taking insects, insect eggs and larva. The abundance of scales on the sycamore tree may be one reason it seems to prefer this tree and accompanying vegetation.

Just over five inches long, the Yellow-throated Warbler has a blue-gray back and tail. Two white wing bars are prominent. The underside is white with a bright-yellow throat. Heavy, black streaks mark the flanks. The head sports a black crown with white eye-stripe. The cheek is black with a white patch at the back edge of the cheek, adjoining the neck. A partial white eye-ring is present under the eye and Florida birds have yellow lores in the eye-stripe. It sings loudly from the top of trees and can be heard from a good distance. The song is a *swee swee swee swee swee-ter* somewhat reminiscent of the Yellow Warbler with the last notes speeded up slightly and rising in pitch.

In Florida, nests are often made in Spanish moss when available. Otherwise they will be placed on a horizonal branch of a tree, usually a pine or live oak and can be anywhere from ten to a hundred feet from the ground. When the nest is in Spanish moss, the bulk of the nest is the moss and it is lined with fine grass and plant down. The tree limb nests are built from bark, weed stems, grasses and are lined with small grasses and plant down.

Four light-colored eggs marked with a variety of colors are incubated for about two weeks by the female. It is uncertain who attends the young and how long it takes for them to fledge; it is thought that it is about two weeks. In the northern part of its range, one brood is produced; two are common in Florida.

Yellow-throated Warbler

Palm Warbler   *Dendroica palmarum*

The Palm Warbler is a winter resident of Florida as well as a transient on its way to the Caribbean for the winter or back north into Canada to nest. Except for the southern coastal states, Florida (where it winters) and Wisconsin, Michigan and Minnesota where it nests in the United States, this bird is considered a migrant. In Florida, it is quite abundant during the winter and can be found nearly anywhere there are some trees, shrubs and grass. It is not a timid bird and will feed on the backyard grass or in a park or city lot as long as there is some cover nearby. It can be found in suburbia, on agricultural lands, in state and city parks and preserves as well as a variety of wastelands. The wintering habitat can be dry or moist, wooded or open. In other words, most anyplace will do. In southern Florida it often can be seen feeding on the ground under palm trees or even in the palm tree. It is possible that this habit of feeding in palms is the reason for its name.

The Palm Warbler is a pretty little bird at about five inches tall, but not very noticeable. It appears, on first glance, to be just another sparrow as it flits about the grass looking for insects. However, unlike the Sparrow, the Palm Warbler constantly wags its tail and a closer look will show a bright-yellow breasted bird with muted red-brown streaking. The back is a brown-color with a yellow cast to it. The cap is rusty-red with a buff-yellow eye-stripe. The rusty cap is more noticeable in breeding birds than winter visitors. The undertail coverts are an unstreaked, bright-yellow. The upper tail coverts are somewhat yellow but not as bright as that of the Yellow-rumped Warbler.

Another tail-wagger that may be seen in Florida is the Prairie Warbler which is about the same size and color but is more yellow-colored overall and the streaking on the breast is black instead of brown. Yet another is the Kirtland's Warbler, one of the rarest warblers. Although it is most unlikely that this bird will be seen in Florida about a dozen reports have been filed reporting sightings of this bird in migration.

Palm Warbler

Common Yellowthroat   *Geothlypis trichas*

The Common Yellowthroat, along with the Yellow Warbler, has adapted to a variety of habitats because of the loss of its native wetlands in the United States. The Common Yellowthroat is found all over the United States as a breeding bird and is a permanent resident in the southern coastal states from the mid-Atlantic to California. Normally the Common Yellowthroat prefers wet marsh and shrub lands to nest and forage, in and even today is quite common in these habitats. But, it has also learned to use the drier shrub lands and even forest edges and is becoming a regular in well-landscaped yards and parks.

The Common Yellowthroat is a very tiny warbler, at just five inches, but he makes himself known both by his color and call. His back is dark-olive with a yellow cast and his underside is a bright yellow. The Common Yellowthroat does not have streaks, as does the Yellow Warbler which can be found in the same area. The male has a black mask that is bordered by a light-gray. The female lacks the mask and instead has a faint white eye-ring. Juvenile males have the eye-ring with a faint mask.

The call of the Common Yellowthroat is a loud *witchity witchity witchity* that the male gives frequently during the day. In a cattail marsh, it easy to see the males sitting on the tip of a cattail head, singing with their heads tipped back and just letting loose with all their might. The call note is also distinctive, a sort of deep *chuck*, which does not sound as if it should come from such a small and pretty bird.

Nests are well-hidden, usually at the base of a dense bunch of shrubs; they are very difficult to locate. In a cattail marsh, they will be at the base of a bunch of cattails or thick marsh vegetation. The nest is woven with grasses, weed stems, bark strips and marsh ferns. The inner nest is lined with finer grasses, hair and fine bark strips. The female does the nest constructing and incubates the eggs.

The five creamy-white eggs are marked with brown flecks and hatch in about twelve days. The young grow extremely fast being fed a diet of insects by both parents and fledge in about ten to eleven days. Even after leaving the nest the young will be fed by the parents for a significant amount of time. Two broods are the norm in the south and even in parts of the north because of the short turnaround time from nest building to fledging. Nesting in Florida begins in April, about the time as the rest of North America except the far North. The second brood is on its own by the end of June.

Common Yellowthroat
Female (bottom)   Male (top)

Red-winged Blackbird   *Agelaius phoeniceus*

It has been said that the Red-winged Blackbird is the most numerous bird east of the Mississippi River. This is probably true because of the varying habitats in which the Redwing nests. In Florida it is considered a permanent resident. The resident populations are increased during the winter with migrants from the North. The Red-winged Blackbird prefers marshes and shrubby wetlands. But over the years it has learned to adapt to a variety of habitats including old fields, forest edges, river valleys, parks, agricultural lands and our suburban yards.

The male is aptly named, having a entirely black body with red epaulets, or patches, on the shoulders of the wings. The red is bordered by a narrow stripe of yellow. The male can control the amount of the epaulets it shows. When on display in defense of a female or territory the red patch will be quite raised and showy.

A rather large bird at between eight and nine inches, the Red-wing has a very pointed, black bill used to capture and eat insects, its main diet. The female is a dark-streaked brown above and lighter on the underside with heavy streaking. She has a tan cheek patch below a brown eye-stripe, above which is a tan eye-stripe. Immature males resemble the females but have some of the red wing patch evident.

The nest is usually placed in dense marsh vegetation where it emerges from the water. In brushy areas it will be placed in a shrub or dense herbaceous plants. The nest is made of grasses, sedges, rushes and mosses intertwined with standing vegetation. The inner nest is lined with the same material except that it is finer.

In the marsh, the male Red-wing Blackbird has a harem of females in his territory. Each female builds her own nest and incubates the eggs for about twelve days. The eggs are a pale-green with dark markings ranging from brown to purple. Four eggs are produced in each nest. Both adults feed the young a diet of insects for about two weeks at which time they are ready to leave. Being born over water for the most part, the young birds are pretty adept at survival and are able to swim in less than a week. In Florida nesting begins in April and two to three broods are produced.

In winter huge flocks of northern migrants converge on Florida and mix with the local populations. On occasion they may become a nuisance or be harmful to crops. The wintering birds eat more seeds and grain than during the summer which makes it easy to attract this colorful bird to a feeding station. Adult males leave the wintering grounds first, followed by adult females, then the immature birds. In the north, the return of the Red-wing Blackbird can be one of the first signs of spring.

Red-winged Blackbird
Female (right)   Male (left)

Boat-tailed Grackle and Common Grackle

Quiscalus major and Quiscalus quiscula

Florida is the permanent home to two of the three Grackles found in the United States: the Common Grackle and Boat-tailed Grackle. The Common Grackle likes areas that have scattered trees, such as park land and suburbia. It has adapted well to agricultural areas as well as backyards and birdfeeding handouts.

The Common Grackle is twelve inches long and is a black bird with a purplish sheen on its head and a bronze metallic sheen on the rest of its body. The eye of the Common Grackle is a light-yellow which is striking against the dark-purplish head. The sexes are similar in appearance but the female is a bit smaller and her tail is not as keel-shaped. The tail is rather long and in flight makes a keel-shaped wedge.

The Boat-tailed Grackle is a large bird at a foot-and-a-half for males and fifteen inches for females. The tail on this Grackle is long and fans out dramatically. The Florida birds have brown eyes instead of the yellow of the Atlantic coast birds. The female is a rust-brown all over with lighter-brown on the head, neck and chest. The tail in the female is much shorter and not as fancy.

In Florida, the Boat-tailed Grackle likes coastal marshes and waterways. Inland from the coast it still prefers wetlands but can also be found in open areas. It has adapted, along with the Common Grackle, to take advantage of agricultural practices and will follow a tractor turning the soil looking for exposed morsels to eat. In coastal marshes, it feeds on crayfish, worms, snails, fish and a variety of aquatic invertebrates. It will feed in the shallow waters as well as the wet margins by walking up and down the beach.

Nesting begins in February for the Boat-tailed Grackle and it may raise a brood or two in the spring. It also nests in the fall. Like the Red-winged Blackbird, nests are usually placed in emergent vegetation but it will also build nests in trees. The Boat-tailed Grackle is a colonial nester, forming loose colonies in which the males are outnumbered two-to-one. Females build the nest and incubate the eggs for two weeks when both parents take care of the young until fledging two weeks later.

The Common Grackle begins nesting in March when it builds a nest in a relatively dense tree or shrub. Nest sites are usually near water and they may even place them over water like the Red-winged Blackbird. Both types of Grackles make a fairly bulky nest that is lined with mud which itself is lined with fine plant material. The female builds the nest and incubates the five green-white eggs for two weeks. Baby birds take about three weeks to fledge and for another few days they will be still begging from the parents. Common Grackles will have two broods in Florida.

Boat-tailed Grackle (upper left) Female, brown head   **Common Grackle (lower right)**

Orchard Oriole *Icterus spurius*

The Orchard Oriole is a permanent breeding resident of north Florida as well as a migrant on its way to South America for the winter or back to the United States to breed. Although it breeds in the north only, the breeding range is expanding southward into Florida.

In Florida, the Orchard Oriole prefers open woodlands, forest edges, park lands and suburban areas. Often this bird can be found feeding and nesting at stream sides where it forages along the edge. It is almost never found in a dense forest. The Orchard Oriole eats insects and occasionally berries. They can sometimes be enticed to take nectar from a feeder.

The male Orchard Oriole is a brick-red overall with a black head, tail and wings. It has a faint buff-colored wingbar and the bill and legs are black. The female is an olive-green above and a greenish-yellow below. The wing of the female is a light-brown or olive-brown with two white wingbars.

The song of the Orchard Oriole resembles that of a Northern Oriole but is more rapid and varied. The song is a variety of loud whistles and chortles that seem to come from deep within. The song is short and to the point with a drop at the end. A quick *wheer* at the end of the call can help in identification.

The nest of the Orchard Oriole resembles that of the Northern Oriole, although not as long and pendulant. Hung from the fork of a tree branch, it is usually between ten to fifty feet above the ground. The nest is woven with plant fibers including grasses, strings, Spanish moss, hair and strips of fine bark. The nest is cupped but not as deeply as the Northern Oriole. The cup is lined with fine, downy material and grasses. The Orchard Oriole will hide the hanging nest by intertwining it with hanging leaves and small branches. Many times it is well-hidden in a hanging clump of Spanish moss.

Markings on the eggs may be brown, purple or any gradation between them. The overall color of the egg is a light-blue to white. Four to five eggs are laid in the nest and incubated by the female for nearly two weeks. The young birds are fed a heavy diet of insects and fledge in about another two weeks. Both parents attend the young and many times they will remain together as a family group well into the fall. In certain parts of the United States these birds appear to nest in groups.

Orchard Oriole
Male (bottom)   Female (top)

Northern Cardinal *Cardinalis cardinalis*

Probably no bird creates more excitement at a backyard feeding station than the Northern Cardinal. It is common throughout Florida. Its preferred habitat is the edges of forested areas, brushy areas, park lands, cemeteries and increasingly the suburban back yard. Even though the Northern Cardinal is considered permanent residents, an influx of northern-raised birds will move into Florida for the winter.

The male Cardinal is bright-red allover, including his bill, with a black mask and pronounced crest. The female is predominantly buff-brown with red on the wings, crest, breast, tail and bill. Juveniles lack the red bill and are browner overall. The bill is sharply-pointed and resembles a short ice-cream cone. The massive bill is used to crush seeds.

The song of the Northern Cardinal is a loud and cheerful *what-cheer what-cheer what-cheer cheer cheer cheer wheet wheet wheet purdy purdy purdy*, or any combination of these. In certain locales very specific dialects are learned. In one small village in the Smoky Mountains male Northern Cardinals are supposed to be saying *whirlpool whirlpool whirlpool*. As permanent residents, the Cardinals are among the first birds to sing during the spring. There are three birds from which you can learn the *chip* notes: the Yellow-rumped Warbler, the Common Yellowthroat and the Northern Cardinal. The *chip* is sharp and fairly loud. As the Northern Cardinal moves around and feeds, they use this *chip* to keep track of each other. The Cardinal does it often, and once you have learned it, you will not forget it.

Courtship rituals of the Northern Cardinals are interesting. Both sexes sing, but the female is softer and accompanies the male. When courtship begins the male entices her with a seed morsel, which she takes from his mouth. Many would call this kissing. Occasionally you will see these paired birds with crests raised singing softly together and swaying back and forth as in a staged duet.

The Cardinal will build its nest in a shrub or small tree. Typically the nest will be about four to six feet from the ground, occasionally ten to twelve feet. The nest is well-hidden but loosely built of twigs, weed stems, bark, grasses, leaves and roots. The inner nest is lined with hair and fine grasses. Three to five bluish-green eggs marked with brown are normal for the nest. Incubation is shared by both parents for about twelve days. Young are fed a variety of insects, seeds, berries and fruit. The young will leave the nest in about twelve days. Up to four broods are raised in Florida, less in the north. While the female is on a second nest the male will continue to feed fledged young.

Northern Cardinal
Female (bottom)   Male (top)

Indigo Bunting   *Passerina cyanea*

The Indigo Bunting, at just over five inches long, is a common nesting species in northern Florida and a winter resident in central and southern Florida. Most Indigo Buntings travel on to Mexico and Central America in April and May and again in August to October. The Indigo Bunting seems to be expanding its breeding range southward into Florida.

The male Indigo Bunting has the typical conical finch bill and is a deep-blue over its entire body. The bill is gray. In low light these males may appear completely black. The female is dull-brown overall and has a buff-colored breast with brown streaks. Her back has no discernable streaking. The wings and tail of the female have a hint of blue in them. Immature birds resemble the female.

The Indigo Bunting male sings from a high perch all summer long. The song is paired phrases, usually in twos, but occasionally in threes, given in a series. A common mnemonic is *fire fire where where here here put it out quick put it out quick.*

The Indigo Bunting's habitat is open weed fields and grasslands with sporadic trees and tangle, woodland edges, park lands, railroad right-of-ways and fence rows along agricultural fields that are not manicured.

While the male Indigo Bunting is singing high up on his perch, the female is building the nest. Brambles, raspberry bushes and thickets are the preferred nesting sites for this bird. It will also use small shrubs and trees and even corn stalks. The female builds the nest alone from dried grasses, leaves, bark, Spanish moss, snake skins and weeds. Spanish moss is used extensively where available. The oval-to-round nest is lined with rootlets, fine grass, plant down and occasionally, feathers.

The female incubates three to four blue-white eggs, often unmarked. She will incubate the eggs for about two weeks or less. Both adults take care of the young until they fledge ten to twelve days later. The male takes a very active part in the foraging of food for the young. Like the Yellow Warbler, if the female finds the egg of a Cowbird she will cover it over with another nest, killing the cowbird eggs.

The Indigo Bunting is mostly a seed eater but takes a few berries and insects as well. In suburban backyards, the Indigo Bunting male will come to a thistle feeder for the first two to four weeks. To see the blue-colored Indigo Bunting and the yellow American Goldfinch feeding at the same time would be a feast for the eyes! When immature males return to their nesting grounds and during migration, they may appear mottled and very scruffy. They are going through their molt and will be bright-blue in a few short weeks.

Indigo Bunting
Female (top) Male (bottom)

Painted Bunting *Passerina ciris*

The Painted Bunting is one of the most colorful birds that breed in Florida, outside parrot escapees. It breeds in the Atlantic coast counties of northern Florida and the coastal areas along the Atlantic coast as far north as Virginia. On the Gulf coast side there is a gap in the populations of breeding birds and none can found in Alabama and Mississippi; however in Texas it is a fairly common inland breeding bird. In southern Florida, it is a winter resident but is migratory throughout the state, wintering in Mexico and Central America.

Wonderment is the common sentiment at the brilliant array of colors displayed by the Painted Bunting. At just over five inches long, the male Painted Bunting has a bright-blue head, lime-green back, dark wings and tail, bright-red front and rump (top and bottom). It is almost as if this bird was put together by a committee. The female is a dull lime-green on the back and yellow-green on the front. The song of the Painted Bunting is a clear, thin warble that is somewhat sing-songy and a bit drawn out.

The Painted Bunting prefers brushy and thickly-vegetated habitats along forest edges, railroad right-of-ways, fence lines, in backyards, along stream sides and city and state parks. During migration, many people successfully attract this bird to their feeding stations using birdseed. A popular place to find this bird at a feeder is Corkscrew Swamp Sanctuary.

During May the female builds the nest in small trees and shrubs, occasionally in a tangle of ivy or vines. The nest is constructed of grass, soft weeds, leaves and ferns. It is a deep cup, precisely made and is lined with fine grasses and hair. Pale-brown spots concentrate around the large end of a pale gray-white, occasionally bluish, egg. Incubation by the female takes about twelve days. The male and female both tend the young. The young are fed partially-digested regurgitated seeds young and as they near fledging they will be able to take some whole seeds. The young may also eat some insects. Occasionally, the adults will take berries, fruits and insects. In the south, two to three broods are common although four broods have been reported. In the northern part of its range one to two broods are normal.

In migration, the Painting Bunting can be seen in April through the first of June and again from late July through October. Each year there are reports of the Painted Bunting overwintering in central and southern Florida as well as possible breeding birds scattered throughout the state. Wherever they show up they cause excitement because of the combination of their bright colors.

Painted Bunting

Rufous-sided Towhee *Pipilo erythrophthalmus*

The Rufous-sided Towhee is a common year-round resident in Florida. The Rufous-sided Towhee prefers forest edges, open woodlands, wooded parks, stream-side thickets and older wooded suburbs.

The male Rufous-sided Towhee has a black head, tail and upper parts. The tail has large, white corners on the feathers which are very showy in flight. His undersides are white and his flanks are "rufous," a brick-orange color. He has a red eye. The female Rufous-sided Towhee is an elegant chocolate-brown above which makes her quite beautiful in her own right, although not as striking as the male. In Florida, the majority of the Rufous-sided Towhees have white eyes instead of red, but in the Rufous-sided Towhees found in the panhandle have red eyes. However, the eyes vary between different shades of red. During the winter, the red-eyed northern migrants merge with the resident populations.

The call of the Rufous-sided Towhee is *drink your teeee*, but a variety of other combinations are given. Upon arrival to the breeding ground in the spring, it seems as if they need a refresher course. The male may start for a day or so just doing the *drink* call and then, as if remembering, he will add the *your*. By the third or fourth day, he will add *tea* and the call is complete again. Or he may skip a step and just call *drink teeeee*. A good identifying characteristic of the Rufous-sided Towhee is the way it feeds on the forest floor, where it scratches with both feet, raking back the leaves, exposing grubs, seeds and other invertebrates. The Rufous-sided Towhee scratches with both feet together; making a sound that seems much louder as if a huge pile of leaves is being pushed away.

The Rufous-sided Towhee nests in small shrubs, palmettos, on the ground or small thick trees. The female builds the nest out of twigs, grasses, weeds, bark strips and leaves. The interior of the nest is lined with fine hair, grasses and fine-shredded bark. The female incubates the four grayish to creamy-white eggs, marked with brown splotches, for about thirteen days. The brown spots are concentrated on the larger end of the egg. Both sexes attend the young.

The young are fed predominately insects, but berries and fruit are added as they get older. In about twelve days the young are ready to fledge. Nesting begins in April and is usually complete by the end of the summer. In Florida up to three broods may be raised although two are more common. In the northern states only one brood is successful.

Rufous-sided Towhee
Female (top)   Male (bottom)

251

Chipping Sparrow *Spizella passerina*

The Chipping Sparrow is a very common winter resident in Florida; possibly the most abundant winter sparrow. Migrating birds arrive in Florida in October and leave by the end of May to winter in Central America. The Chipping Sparrow is a breeding bird in the panhandle of Florida, but it is not terribly abundant. The preferred habitat of the Chipping Sparrow is open forests, forest edges, old fields and farmsteads. It has become extremely adapted to our parks and suburban backyards.

The Chipping Sparrow, at five-and-a-half inches, is one of the most friendly and sociable of our sparrows. Its crown is a red-rust color accented by a white eye-stripe above the eye and black stripe through the eye. The cheek, neck and front are a light gray in color with no streaks or markings. In winter the cap is somewhat rust-colored but has streaks in it. The back, wings and tail are brown with black markings. The wings have two white wingbars in them. The rump is, like the breast, gray.

The song of the Chipping Sparrow is a quite distinctive long trill. It is a little more raspy and longer and not so sweet as the call of the Northern Junco. The male sits on a small shrub or tree and sings constantly. In suburban backyards, it is a common song during the breeding season.

The Chipping Sparrow nests infrequently in the panhandle of Florida, but when it does it places it nest in small trees and shrubs. In suburbia, it prefers small conifers, and builds its nest only a few feet above the ground. The nest is extremely well-constructed from fine grasses, rootlets and thin weeds. The interior is lined with extremely fine grasses and hair. This nest is so well constructed that it can be found still pretty much intact a year or two later. The female does most of the construction and is helped by the male after nearly complete.

The eggs of the Chipping Sparrow are quite beautiful; they are a bright blue-green color with irregular mahogany-colored markings over the larger end of the egg. The eggs are incubated by the female for about two weeks and the young are then attended by both parents for about ten or eleven days until fledging. The young are fed worms and assorted other insects. Even in the northern part of the Chipping Sparrow's range, two broods will be produced.

In the winter, the diet of the Chipping Sparrow changes to a mixed assortment of insects, seeds and berries. During the mating season, and for most of the summer, their diet is mainly insects. In winter these birds can be found mixed with other wintering sparrows foraging across the countryside. On occasion one or more may even spend the winter in the far reaches of the north.

Chipping Sparrow

Index